Santa Clara County Free Library

REFERENCE

ioch: A Place Of Christians

The chronicles of the history of the Antioch Baptist Church of San Jose, California. A glimpse of Christian African-Americans which began in 1893, through years of prayer, excitement, change, pain, and dedication.

This book is a culmination of research which has examined church records, city records, oral histories, county records, and miscellaneous historical documents.

Harriett Arnold

1993

Published by
Western Book Journal Press
Conrad Mollath & Co. / Printers • Publishers
San Mateo, California

Photograph of Founders

Antioch: A Place Of Christians
Chronicles Of An African-American Church
1893-1993

Antioch:
A Place Of Christians

Harriett Arnold

1993

Published by
Western Book Journal Press
Conrad Mollath & Co. / Printers • Publishers
San Mateo, California

Western Book Journal Press
Conrad Mollath & Co. / Printers • Publishers
San Mateo, California

Limited First Edition 1993
Library of Congress Catalog Card Number 93-060521

ISBN: 0-936029.29.3

Illustrations
Chuck Alexander

Editor
Gloria Weddington

DEDICATION

Let Us Go Into The House Of The Lord

".... and the hour shall be filled

with music with song and praise and prayer,

And the burdens of life shall be lifted

from all who enter there ...."

Church Program, January 3, 1993

Photograph of
Clyde Arbuckle and the Author Harriett Arnold
March 1993

TABLE OF CONTENTS

The History Of Antioch Baptist Church

San Jose, California

	1800-1893	1894-1914	1915-1935	1936-1956	1957-1977	1978-1988	1989-1993
In Search of Freedom	→						
California Trail Blazers		→					
The New City			→				
A Changing San Jose				→			
Civil Rights Movement					→		
Urban Renaissance						→	
A Journey Forward							→

FOREWORD

In keeping with the chosen theme, "Journeying Upon God's Foundation," Ephesians 2:19-22, the Apostle Paul was speaking "to the saints and the faithful in Jesus Christ" everywhere.

In this most impersonal letter, let us be reminded that God addresses each of us in a very personal way. God's spiritual breath will enable you to be "more than conquerors" as you begin your journey into the next century of Antioch History. However, underlying past progress are the words God used to challenge Joshua, "....Thou art old and advanced in years, and there remains yet very much land to be possessed," Joshua 13:1.

In your joy of celebrating one hundred years, enough has not been done or accomplished. We thank God because "we have come this far by faith leaning on the prayers and work of his saints." However, as members of the Body of Christ, "there remains yet much more to be done," if we are to give Him the Glory and without hoping to receive it ourselves.

I urge you to receive the past and arm yourselves for tomorrow because "there remains yet very much to be possessed" for the Glory of God.

**REV. DR. M. SAMUEL PINKSTON
PASTOR EMERITUS, ANTIOCH BAPTIST CHURCH**

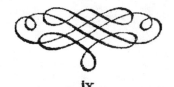

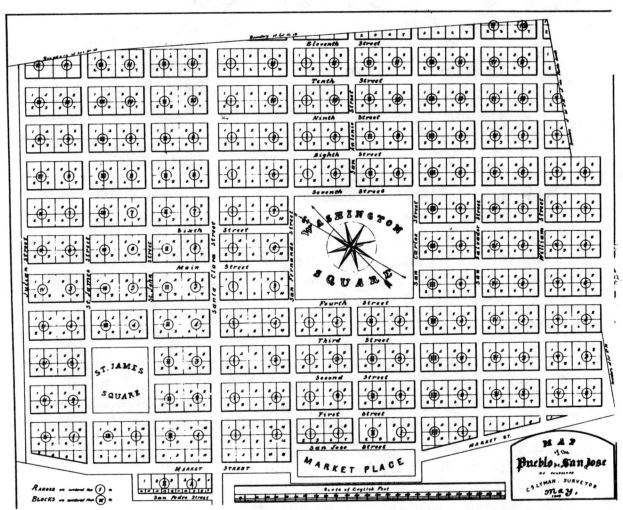

Surveyor Chester S. Lyman first drew a *Plan of the Town of St. Joseph* for
James Stokes in October, 1847, but this *Map of the Pueblo de San José*, made by
the same surveyor in May, 1848, is a finished and larger product. Its accuracy is
unquestioned; its range, block and lot numbers are in use to this day.

Old San Jose
Source: Chester S. Lyman, Surveyor[1]

---

[1] Arbuckle

PREFACE

Franklin D. Roosevelt once said to Americans, "The only thing we have to fear is fear itself."

The founders of the Antioch Baptist Church feared a series of severe social, political, economic, and cultural crisis in 1893. They did not give in to these external forces that may have overwhelmed them, but they believed in the Power of God. They were prayerful and took the steps necessary to establish a legacy for all of us who would follow them.

In the words of Edmund Burke, "people will not look forward to posterity who never look backward to their ancestors."

"Journeying Upon God's Foundation," Ephesians 2:19-22, the theme for the Antioch Church Centennial Celebration, reminds us to be faithful, prayerful, and to always give God the Glory in everything that we do.

We must never forget our ancestors or the legacy they left for each of us.

Author

EDITOR'S NOTE

Antioch: A Place for Christians is a compilation of historical information for African–Americans in the City of San Jose, California and the Antioch Baptist Church. Harriett Arnold is meticulous in detail and reports data and anecdotes obtained from minutes of church business meetings and other library and archival documents.

The contents of this book will appeal to the members of Antioch Baptist Church, other California Christians, and readers interested in the history of African–Americans and their efforts to establish and maintain a place of worship. It is clear from Dr. Arnold's documentation that the church was the center of the African–American spiritual, cultural, educational, and social lives. This has been true since the inception of the African–American church, and remains true today. The church has been the force for social change, political influence and economic stability.

Antioch: A Place for Christians is amazing in its detail; revealing in presentation; logical in organization; and exciting in pictorial representation. This book will fill an open void in the history of African–Americans in Northern California.

Gloria Weddington, Ph.D.

ACKNOWLEDGEMENTS

The history of the Antioch Baptist Church is rich and filled with significant information. A few devout African–American founders have provided the City of San Jose and African–Americans with a rich history and proud traditions.

Our founders have left us with a legacy that has been continued for one hundred years. They were challenged, often irritated, and prayerful that the future of Antioch would be sustained for many years.

It is out of an interest in the history of our ancestors that this book evolved and became reality. This book would not have been possible without all of the assistance provided to the author. Ideas emerged constantly which helped to give shape and direction.

This book bears testimony to the legacy and importance of maintaining our link with the past as we move into the future.

I am especially thankful for all of the assistance received in word processing, editing, photography, librarians, researchers and the many members and friends of the Antioch Baptist Church.

Photograph of Clyde Arbuckle
March 1993

INTRODUCTION

By writing this history of Antioch Baptist Church, Dr. Arnold has filled a long existing vacancy in the religious annals of San José.

She ensured the authenticity of her work by using first sources—oral or written, whenever available.

Moreover, she wished to produce a dependable source for future researchers, as well as, otherwise interested readers.

It must convey to all readers an adequate knowledge of the cultural contributions that the City of San José has received from its citizens of African lineage.

CLYDE ARBUCKLE
Historian
City of San Jose

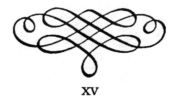

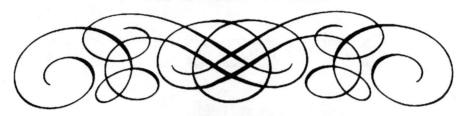

Pastors Of The Antioch Baptist Church

Name  Dates

Name	Dates
Rev. Cyclades C. Laws	1893-1895
Rev. Thomas F. Smith	1895-1897
Rev. W. A. Mitchell	1897-1901
Rev. W. Brown	1901-1903
Rev. Emmett B. Reed	1903-1906
Rev. Robert A. Lewis	1906-1910
Rev. Dr. M. C. McIlvane	1910-1911
Rev. J. W. Wiley	1911-1912
Rev. D. L. Potts	1912-1915
Rev. J. A. Dennis	1915-1917
Rev. G. W. Hill	1917-1919
Rev. William Allen Magette	1920-1939
Rev. T. M. Davis	1940-1946
Rev. C. W. Washington	1946-1973
Rev. Eddie Porter (Interim)	1973-1974
Rev. Dr. M. Samuel Pinkston	1974-1988
Rev. Dr. Arthur Jarrett (Interim)	1989-1990
Rev. Frank L. Selkirk, Sr.	1990-1992
Rev. Richard Nance, Jr. (Interim)	1993

Photograph of the Present Church
March, 1993

CHAPTER I
In Search of Freedom

According to documents translated into English from Spanish, the discovery of California can be traced to Friar Marco and the Negro guide Estevancio, an Arab Negro from Azamore on the Atlantic Coast of Morocco. Estevancio acted as guide and perished during an expedition to New Mexico. He took part in the discovery of the southwestern part of this country, which eventually led to the discovery of California.[1]

An exploring expedition under the direction of Cabeza de Vaca nine years prior to Cortez, took part in a visit to this area of North America. Estevancio was a member of this small expedition which reached Mexico City and told of their strange experiences in this area. In 1535 Cortez discovered California.[2]

Spain settled the California coast in 1769. Missionaries, soldiers, and settlers could be found in California between 1769 and 1846.

San Jose was established as the first *civic pueblo* founded by Lt. Don Jose de Moraga, November 29, 1777.[3]

Source:
Clyde Arbuckle's
History of San Jose

[1]Beasley
[2]Beasley
[3]Arbuckle

Don Jose Joaquin Moraga was ordered to found a settlement at San Jose. There were approximately nine families who set up mud–plastered houses.[3]

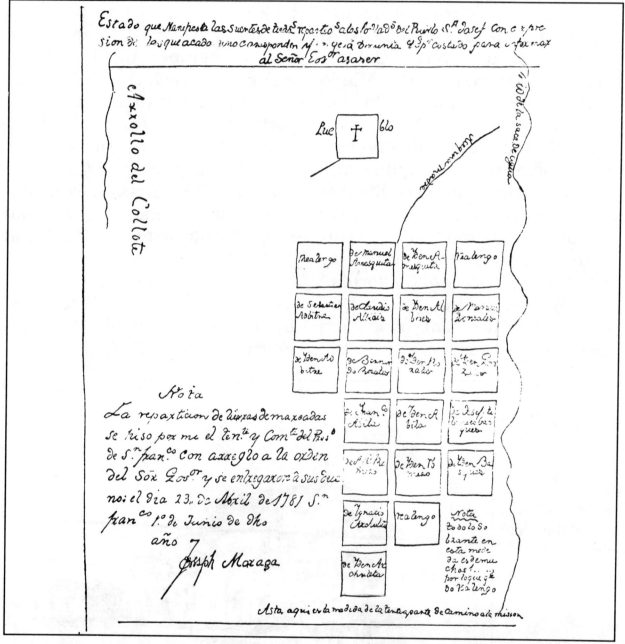

Map of Plough Lands Assigned to the Nine Settlers of San Jose.

---

[3]Lockley

The census *(Padrón)* listed the nine original land grantees of 1783 as follows:

Spaniards, 3;
Coyote (half–breed), 1;
Indian, 1;
Mulattoes 2;
Mestizo (half–breed), 1;
Unknown, 1.

In 1821 Mexico became independent of Spain, and on April 11, 1822, California took the Oath of Allegiance to Mexico's Constitution of 1824.[1] California was an independent Mexican governmental entity and with it came changes to the population. There was a strong influence by the Catholic Church through the establishment of missions throughout the State of California.

There were several priests and missionaries in the state. It was not until 1846 that California was annexed into the United States. There was a mixture of "Hispanics, Indians, Mulattoes, Negroes, and European–Americans."

The Coloma gold discovery of January 24, 1848, brought thousands of people from all over the United States and other countries.[2] There were free slaves and slave owners who brought their slaves with them to California.

By February 28, 1849, the Gold Rush was on as well as the first steamship from the east coast docking in San Francisco with the mail.[3]

". . . . The people of Color, at many points throughout the State, celebrated in a becoming manner the Anniversary of the Emancipation on January 1st."

Source: San Jose Patriot January 6, 1864

---

[1] Arbuckle
[2] Arbuckle
[3] Arbuckle

There were several African-American gold miners who came to California in 1849. The early Black miners often used their earnings to pay for freedom, liberty, their family, and relatives who were far away or to contribute to the Colored Conventions to secure legislation for the African-Americans in California. They were not able to legally own mines, but sold shares of their riches from the gold that had been found in the mines.

Some African-Americans who came to California migrated to San Jose. There are few records which describe the reasons for settling in San Jose, however, a number of individuals can be identified. Archival records indicate eight names of African-Americans who settled in Santa Clara County and San Jose:[1]

Alfred White
H. E. Speight
William Whiting
Mrs. Harriett Smith
James Williams
Ella Hawkins
Jacob Overton
Sarah Massey Overton

San Jose in 1893 was beginning to grow in population. There continued to be a strong Spanish influence but there were European-Americans, Mexicans, and the African-Americans who settled in the City.

Serving the early years of San Jose, there was an African-American church but it was not a Baptist place of worship. Reverend Peter Williams Casey had already established himself with the Trinity Episcopal Church in 1863.[2]

Still another church was the African Methodist Episcopal Zion Church organized in 1864. They contributed to the religious life of African-Americans in San Jose.

Photograph of
Rev. Peter Williams Cassey
(Courtesy of Trinity Espiscopal Church)

[1]Beasley
[2]Trinity Episcopal Church Records

4

San Jose was beginning to grow in 1893 with less than 1% of the population African–Americans.[1]

The January 6, 1893, newspaper stated that "Dr. Washington visits San Jose at Zion A.M.E. from Chicago and there were 3,000 in the audience for this colored evangelist."[2]

January 18, 1893, "A colored man at the El Monte Hotel in Los Gatos decorated the hotel register with original designs in an artistic manner."[3]

On August 2, 1893, the Antioch Baptist Church was organized in the home of Mr. & Mrs. Henry Hawkins.[4] His address was 75 Vine Street.

On August 7, 1893, the Colored Odd Fellows Annual meeting was held on Saturday and Sunday. There was a parade and program. They pitched their tents at Third and Santa Clara.[5]

The following month Reverend C. C. Laws was appointed the pastor of the Church, September 1893.[6]

Each of these events is significant in the chronology of events that eventually led to the organization of the Antioch Baptist Church.

The article about Dr. Washington implies that there was a strong interest in religious speakers in the City. It also implies that in the City of San Jose, this minister had a large audience interested in hearing the Word of God.

The work at the El Monte Hotel is significant in that it illustrates that artistic works were appreciated and valued by the community.

Mr. & Mrs. Hawkins opened their home on August 2, 1893 for the organization of the Church. Approximately five days later, the State convention met in San Jose. Through meetings and discussions at the convention, arrangements were made for future church services to be held in the Odd Fellows Hall in San Jose.

[1]San Jose Directory, 1893
[2]San Jose Evening News, Jan. 6, 1893
[3]San Jose Evening News, Jan. 18, 1893
[4]Antioch Journal, November, 1963
[5]San Jose Evening News, August 7, 1893

[6]Antioch Church Records

Zion African M. E. Church

This Society was organized in 1864 by Deacons William Smith and James Lodge, with eighteen members.

Their Church was erected at Fourth and San Antonio Streets. At present this Church is the only religious organization among the Colored people of this City, and is in a prosperous condition. The attendance on Sunday being always sufficient to fill the Church.

Source: San Jose Mercury News, January 1, 1892

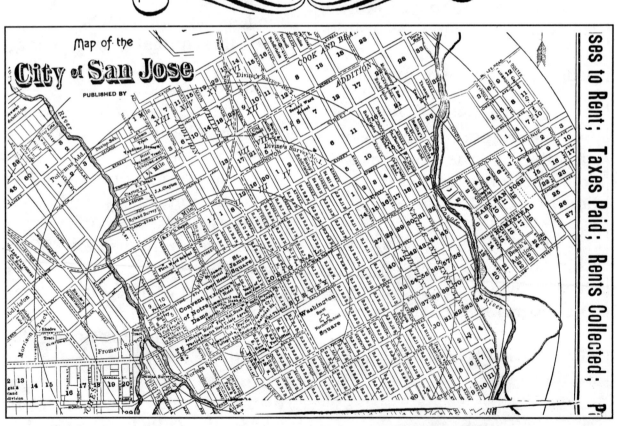

Source: Map of the City of San Jose
James A. Clayton, 1888

230	SAN JOSE DIRECTORY.

Hatch Cora M Miss, res NW cor University and Elm

Hatch Ephraim, capitalist, res NW cor University and Elm

Hatch Isaac A, carpenter, res 741 15th

Hatch Jackson, atty at law, Porter Building, rm 50, res Alumn Rock ave nr Hale ave, East San Jose

Hatch Jas M, res 12th nr Empire

Hatch Jas N, blacksmith, res 229 E Santa Clara

Hatch Jas O, painter, res 12th nr Empire

Hatch Wm D, orchardist, res Berryessa, P O San Jose

HATCHER CHARLES M, real estate and insurance, 27 E Santa Clara, res 117 N 5th

Hathaway R E Mrs, res 384 S 2d

Hatman Annie Miss, res 248 S 7th

Hatman Fredk D, res 248 S 7th

Hattabough Fred, fruit dealer, Alumn Rock ave nr Jones ave, res Calhoun nr Clay, East San Jose

Hattabough Isaac J, mfr boss gopher trap, res Calhoun nr Clay, East San Jose

Hatton Sarah A Mrs, furnished rooms, 34 S 3d, res same

Haub Jacob, bartender Graessle & Geoffroy, res 371 W San Carlos

Haub Theodore G, butcher F Hauer, res 371 W San Carlos

Hauck M G Miss, res 380 E San Salvador

Hauenstein Henry, capitalist, res 260 Latewana

Hauenstein Jacob, res 260 Latewana

Hauenstein John W, res 260 Latewana

Hauenstein Minnie C Miss, res 260 Latewana

HAUER FRANZ, proprietor Capital Meat Market, 89 E San Fernando, res 368 W San Carlos

Haufmann John, machinist, res 455 S 2d

Hauser Chas, carpenter, res McLaughlin ave nr Whitton ave, East San Jose

Hauser Frank X, chainman city engineer, res 263 E St John

Hauss Fredk W, brewer Eagle Brewery, res 416 W San Carlos

Haussler Otto, photographer, removed to Oakland, Cal

HAUSSLER PAUL PROF, superior photographer and portrait artist, 68 S 1st, res 148 S 2d

Havens Amanda Mrs, res 620 S 3d

Havens Truman, died Dec, 1892

Hawkins Henry, stableman Occidental Stable, res 75 Vine

Hawkins Irene Miss, res 211 S 8th

Hawkins Rufus L, steam fitter, res Fairbrother ave nr Alumn Rock ave, East San Jose

Hawley E Mrs, millinery, 16 E San Fernando, res same

Hawley Elijah H, res 16 E San Fernando

Hawley Fred W (W G Hawley & Co) res 850 Spring

Hawley G A, driver San Jose Gurney Cab Co, res 430 N 5th

San Jose City Directory 1893

Drawing Circa
Source: Sign Posts 1889-90[2]

Life in San Jose in 1893 was difficult for African–Americans. Weathering the hard–life in this new land on the edge of California was not easy.

The location of the Church on Julian Street was in the Second Ward, known as Tar Flats. It was described as a working class neighborhood, centered around Tenth and Julian Streets.

According to Harry Farrell, there were two reasons for the name "Tar Flats." One, the name came from an ill–smelling tar weed which grew rampant in the area. Second, the name reflected the fact that the four or five Black families lived there.[1]

---

[1]Farrell, Harry
[2]Loomis, Patricia

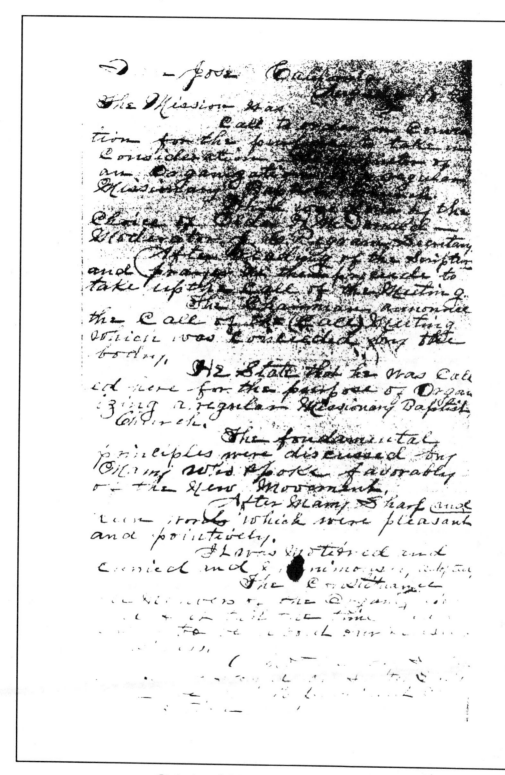

Original Minutes, August 2, 1893

Original Minutes, September 4, 1893

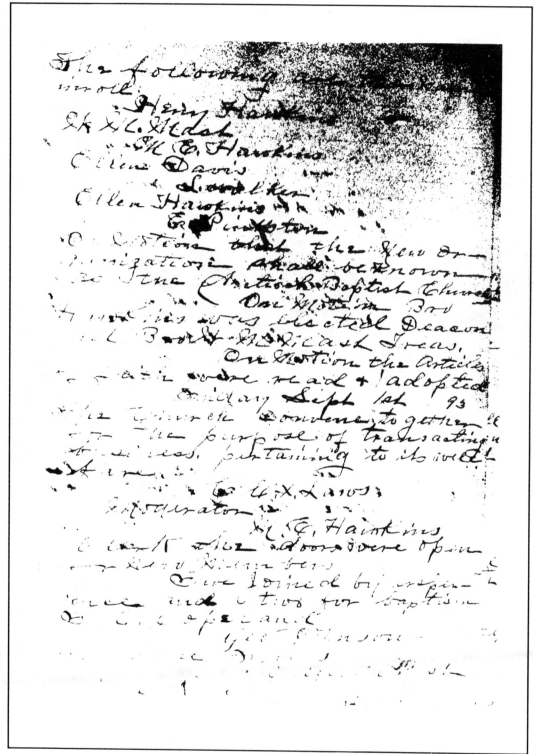

Original Church Minutes, September 4, 1893

Source: Early Day San Jose
Frances Fox

Dash Away Stables
Early San Jose ~ 1885

The San Jose Directory shows that Mr. Henry Hawkins was a stableman at the Occidental Stables. During this period before the automobile the position of stableman was an important job for a man in the City. The photograph on this page depicts one of the several stables that could be found in the City.

Members of Antioch Baptist Church visited other churches in San Francisco and Oakland. The primary mode of transportation was by horse and buggy.

CHAPTER II
California Trail Blazers

San Jose, September 4, 1893 –

The Antioch Baptist Church of this City met at the above date for the purpose of transacting business. The house was called to order at 8:20 p.m. with Rev. C. C. Laws as moderator. The meeting was opened by singing Hymn No. 1, after which prayer was offered led by Rev. Laws, followed by singing. The meeting was thus prayerfully opened for business. Different things were discussed in regard to the officers of the Church. Carried that the brothers take Rev. Laws into another room to find out if, and what he would preach for us for. After a good deal of discussion by the sisters, Brother Johnson was elected temporary moderator. The brothers returned. Rev. Laws stated that he would stay in San Jose and preach for them for $10.00 per month and board and as the church grows in number that his salary be increased also. All of the members were pleased with that proposition. And it was moved that he be called as pastor of the Antioch Baptist Church, which motion was unanimously carried.

Antioch Baptist Church was organized Aug. 2, 1893, in the home of Mr. & Mrs. Hawkins. The following month Rev. C. C. Laws became the first pastor of a proud and humble church.

Rev. C. C. Laws would serve as Pastor of Antioch Baptist Church from 1893-1895. The early pioneers of the small church met the first few months in the Odd Fellows Hall:

San Jose Directory, 1894

262   SAN JOSE DIRECTORY.

Lavoie Martin, r 453 S 11th
Law Geo, laborer H Dutard, r S C & L G road nr Williams road
Law Horace C, restaurant Alum Rock Springs, r same
Law Library, W B Hardy pres, Mrs G H Baker librarian, Porter Building
Lawlor Lionel L, bartender W H Green, r 117 N 1st
Lawlor Mamie, domestic 455 S 3d
Lawrence B M Mrs, teacher Newhall St Kindergarten, r Newhall nr Union av
Lawrence C Mrs, r 434 S 10th
Lawrence Chas S, r 216 N 10th
Lawrence Geo, marker S J Laundry Assn, r 279 N 9th
Lawrence Hattie Miss, r 216 N 10th
Lawrence Jas M, orchardist, r Jones av SW cor Jefferson
Lawrence John D, comp J B Carey & Co, r Jones av SW cor Jefferson
Lawrence Libbie G Mrs, r Polhemus NW cor Walnut
Lawrence Milton L, clerk Farmers' Union, r Newhall nr Union av
Lawrence Ora Miss, student, r 281 E San Fernando
Lawrence S M, street sprinkler, r Palm nr Summer
Lawry Jas, saloon Almaden road 1½ m south city limits, r same
Lawry Robt, blacksmith M Broedel, r 771 Orchard
Laws C C N Rev, pastor Antioch Baptist Church, r SW cor 6th and Julian
Lawson Annie Miss, r 1267 S 1st
Lawson Chas B, butcher V Cauhape, r 616 S 7th
Lawson Edwin R, shoes 87 N 1st, r 1267 S 1st
Lawson Geo, painter, r 87 N 14th
Lawson John O, broom mfr 727 Orchard, r same
Lawson Sarah C Miss, r 226 Terraine
Lawton Margaret Mrs, r McLaughlin nr Shortridge av
Layton Emmet, laborer, r 625 Orchard
Layton Frank, pressman, r 642 S 1st
Layton Jas W, orchardist, r cor Pine and Washington av
Layton Louis F, laborer, r 625 Orchard
Layton Patrick J, blacksmith, r 642 S 1st
Layton Teresa E Miss, r 625 Orchard
Lazier Annie Mrs, lodgings 511 S Market
Lazier Desire, groceries 509 S Market, r same
Lazzarini A, orchardist, r Pedro nr Lincoln av
Leabert Thos, saloon Julian NW cor Montgomery, r 507 W Julian
Leach Annie Miss, r 353 S 9th
Leach Edith Miss, teacher Willow Glen District School, r 353 S 9th
Leach Edward, laborer Wm Stevens
Leach Edwin A, farmer, r 630 Delmas av
Leach Sherman H, r 630 Delmas av
Leach Sylvanus, laborer Wm Stevens

SAN JOSE DIRECTORY. 21

GARDEN CITY BANK AND TRUST CO.—99 South 1st. Capital, $300,000. R. McComas, president; T. F. Morrison, cashier.

SECURITY SAVINGS BANK—11 South 1st; W. D. Tisdale, president; A. King, vice president; L. G. Naismith, secretary.

UNION SAVINGS BANK—1st SE cor. Fountain. Authorized capital, $1,000,000; paid up capital, $300,000. H. W. Wright, president and manager; H. W. Edwards, vice president; A. Friant, cashier; F. V. Wright, assistant cashier and secretary.

BANDS.

Conterno's Fifth Regiment Band, Letitia Building.
Schubert's Band, 63 West Santa Clara.

CEMETERIES.

Calvary Cemetery—Alum Rock avenue nr. Capitol avenue; W. Sax sexton.
Oak Hill Cemetery—Monterey road, 1½ miles south limits; H. B. Burns superintendent.

CHURCHES.

BAPTIST.

Antioch—A. O. U. W. Hall. Rev. C. C. X. Laws pastor; Sunday services 11 A. M. and 7:30 P. M.; Sunday school 3 P. M.; prayer meeting Thursday 7:30 P. M.

Emanuel—East SW cor. Crandall. Rev. J. Barr pastor; Sunday services 11 A. M. and 7:30 P. M.; Sunday school 12:15 P. M.; B. Y. P. U. 6:30 P. M.; prayer meeting Thursday 7:30 P. M.

First—2d near cor. San Antonio. Rev. F. M. Mitchell pastor; Sunday services 11 A. M. and 7:30 P. M.; Sunday school 10 A. M.; B. Y. P. U. 6:15 P. M.; prayer meeting Thursday 7:30 P. M.

Swedish—San Carlos near cor. Orchard. Sunday services 11 A. M.

CATHOLIC.

St. Joseph's—Market near cor. San Fernando. Rev. Father D. J. Mahoney pastor; Sunday services 6, 7, 8:15, 9:15 and 10:30 A. M.; Sunday school 9 A. M.; vespers 7:30 P. M.

St. Mary's—3d near Reed. Rev. Father P. I. Miller pastor; Sunday services 8 and 10:30 A. M.

St. Patrick's—Santa Clara NW cor. 9th. P. McGuire pastor; Sunday services 8 and 10:30 A. M. and 7:30 P. M.

San Jose and Santa Clara County Directory 1894

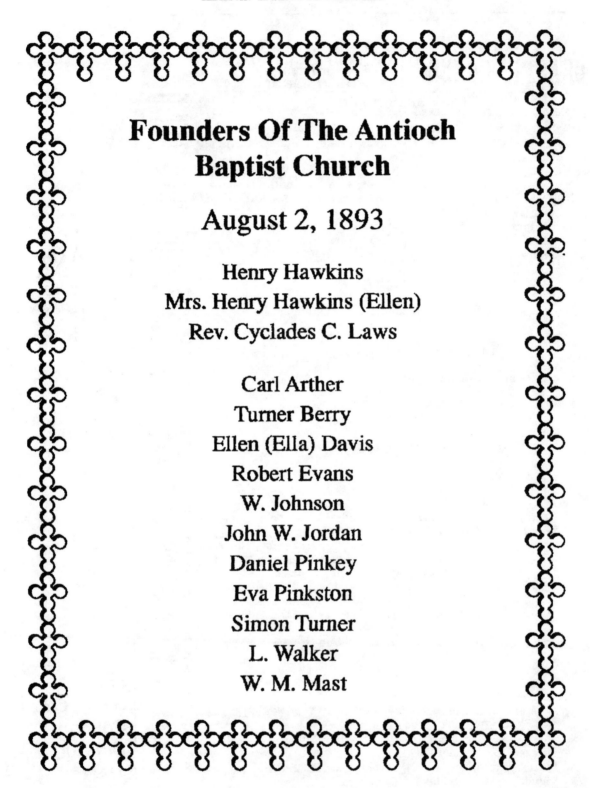

Founders Of The Antioch Baptist Church

August 2, 1893

Henry Hawkins
Mrs. Henry Hawkins (Ellen)
Rev. Cyclades C. Laws

Carl Arther
Turner Berry
Ellen (Ella) Davis
Robert Evans
W. Johnson
John W. Jordan
Daniel Pinkey
Eva Pinkston
Simon Turner
L. Walker
W. M. Mast

Founders Of The Antioch Baptist Church

New Members Joining The Church

September 4, 1893

F. C. Copeland

Josephine Simms

Willie Reno

Annie Fallie

Hattie Johnson

George Johnson

Elizabeth Mast

20   SAN JOSE DIRECTORY.

Rucker District—G. W. Jones, clerk; Gilroy.

San Antonio District—J. McClellan, clerk; Lida C. Clark, teacher; Cupertino.

San Felipe District—C. R. Willson, clerk; Ida M. Moore, teacher; Gilroy.

San Isabel District—R. S. De Forest, clerk; Ellen Heckman, teacher; De Forest.

San Tomas District—M. Ross, clerk; Robert Loosemore, teacher; Campbell.

San Ysidro District—J. F. Phegley, clerk; John Tathman, principal; Nellie Rice, teacher; Gilroy.

Santa Clara District—A. L. Kellogg, clerk; John Manzer, principal; Mina Cole, Ella Glendenning, Loma Jordon, Nannie W. Teaford, Minnie L. Mackay, Kate Doyle, Mrs. A. H. Post, Fannie Fowler, Carrie M. Thompson, teachers; Santa Clara.

Saratoga District—F. M. Farwell, clerk; Carrie Wooster, principal; Mrs. S. F. Whitehurst, Grace Ward, teachers; Saratoga.

Sierra District—Columbus Smith, clerk; L. May Evans, teacher; Berryessa.

Soda Springs District—E. Thomas, clerk; Mary Koeber, teacher; Madrone.

Summit District—F. W. Chase, clerk; W. H. Sisson, teacher; Wrights.

Union District—Mrs. Annie McCarthy, clerk; Ida Waltenspiel, teacher; Los Gatos.

Uvas District—Antonio Montoya, clerk; Blanch Wendt, teacher; New Almaden.

Valley View District—Mrs. C. W. Childs, clerk; Beatrice Childs, teacher; San Jose.

Vineland District—Noah G. Rogers, clerk; Mrs. Lucie Huey, teacher; Los Gatos.

Whisman District—Jas. A. Huff, clerk; Edgar F. Plyler, teacher; Mountain View.

Willow Glen District—C. W. Cuttler, clerk; Mary Bird, principal; Edith Leach, Mildred Hanson, Annie L. Adams, teachers; San Jose.

BANKS.

BANK OF SAN JOSE (THE)—1st NE cor. Santa Clara; T. E. Beans, president; W. K. Beans, vice president; C. T. Park, cashier.

COMMERCIAL AND SAVINGS BANK OF SAN JOSE (THE)—Santa Clara NW cor. 1st; B. D. Murphy, president and manager; J. W. Findlay, vice president; H. Philip, secretary; J. T. McGeoghegan, cashier.

FIRST NATIONAL BANK OF SAN JOSE (THE)—SW cor. Santa Clara and 1st; W. D. Tisdale, president, A. King, vice president; L. G. Nesmith, cashier.

San Jose and Santa Clara County Directory 1894

Antioch: A Place Of Christians

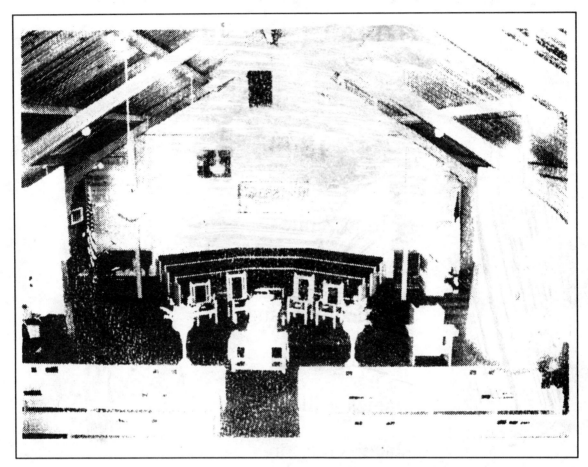

Photograph of the Present Church
March 1993
Source: Antioch Church Records

Pioneer African–American Families of Santa Clara County

1849

Alfred White

H. E. Speight

William Whiting

Harriett Smith

James Williams

Jacob Overton

Sara Massey Overton

*Ella Hawkins[1]

---

*First Black woman of record in Santa Clara County.
[1]Beasley

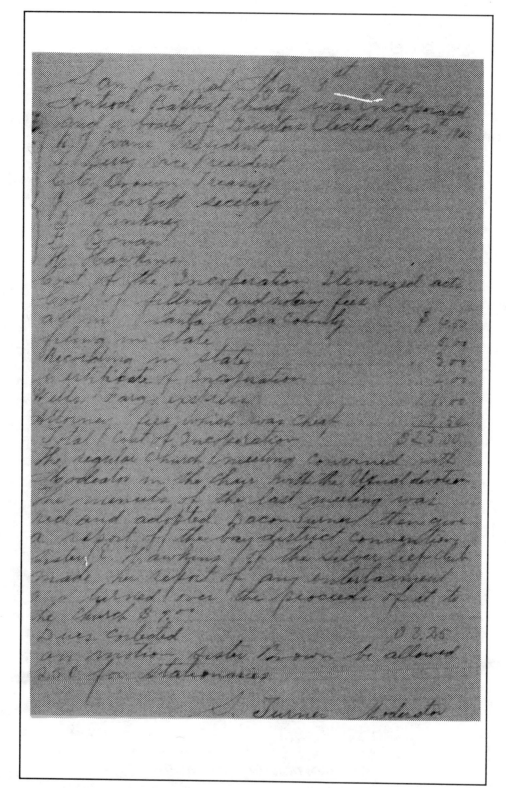

Incorporation of Antioch Baptist Church
1905

On April 28, 1905, Antioch Baptist church incorporated with the first Board of Trustees. They were:

Turner Berry
F. Bowman
C. C. Brown
J. C. Corbett
R. J. Evans
Henry Hawkins
Daniel Pinkey

A copy of the Resolution Certificate on file was signed by the Reverend J. Morgan, Moderator, and John M. Collins, Recording Secretary and it is attested with the Seal of the General Baptist Association of California on November 1, 1906.

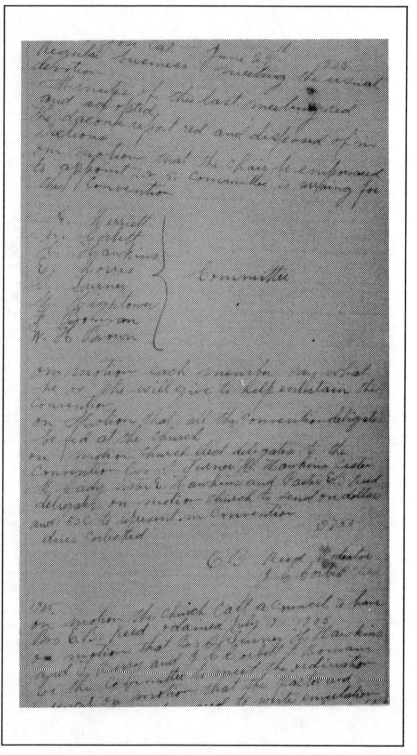

Incorporation of Antioch Baptist Church
1905

Resolutions of the members of the Antioch Baptist Ch. of San Jose, a religious corporation.

WHEREAS the Antioch Baptist Church of San Jose, a religious Corporation is the owner in fee of the following described real property, to-wit:

All that certain lot, piece or parcel of land situate in the City of San Jose, County of Santa Clara, State of California, and bounded and described as follows, to-wit:

Commencing at a point on the Southerly line of Julian Street distant 105 feet 9 inches from the intersection of the Southerly line of Julian Street with the Easterly line of Sixth Street, and running thence Easterly and along the Southerly line of Julian Street 31 feet 9 inches; thence at right angles Southerly and parallel to Sixth Street 68 feet 9 inches; thence at right angles Westerly and parallel to Julian Street 31 feet 9 inches; thence at right angles Northerly and parallel to Sixth Street 68 feet 9 inches to the place of beginning, and being the property deeded by Dora Cohen and Mark Cohen to Mary Farrell by deed dated July 27th, 1882, said deed being recorded August 3rd, 1882 in Liber 64 of Deeds page 199, Records of said Santa Clara County, to which said deed and record reference is hereby made for a more complete discription.

Above: Incorporation of Antioch Baptist Church
1905

Baptist Church of San Jose, a religious corporation, by a mortgage or deed of trust upon said above described property and the improvements thereon, executed by said Antioch Baptist Church of San Jose, a religious corporation, or by its duly and legally constituted and acting officer or officers.

BE IT THEREFORE RESOLVED by us, the members and governing body of said Antioch Baptist Church of San Jose, a religious corporation, that the said Antioch Baptist Church of San Jose, a religious corporation, borrow the sum of $1100 for the purpose of paying, satisfying and discharging said indebtedness incurred as aforesaid, and that the repayment of said sum of $1100 to be borrowed be secured by a mortgage or deed of trust upon said above described real property and the improvements erected by the Antioch Baptist Church of San Jose, a religious corporation, or by its duly and legally constituted and acting officer or officers, and

BE IT FURTHER RESOLVED that Board of Directors of said Antioch Baptist Church of San Jose, a religious corporation, take in behalf of said Antioch Baptist Church of San Jose, a religious corporation, and the members thereof, such steps as shall be legal and necessary to procure said loan of $1100 for the purposes aforesaid and to enable said Antioch Baptist Church of San Jose, a religious corporation, to properly and legally execute a mortgage or deed of trust upon said property and the improvements there-

Above: Resolution of Incorporation
1905

Horse Car Days   *Source: Early Day San Jose, Frances Fox*

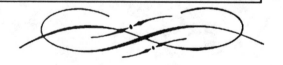

San Jose Directory, 1870

THE

SAN JOSE CITY DIRECTORY

AND

Business Guide of Santa Clara Co.

FOR THE

YEAR COMMENCING JANUARY 1, 1870,

BEING A

COMPLETE DIRECTORY OF THE RESIDENTS WITHIN
THE CITY OF SAN JOSE;

ALSO, A FULL DIRECTORY OF

Public Offices, Streets, Avenues, &c.

TOGETHER

WITH A CAREFULLY ARRANGED INDEX TO THE SYSTEM OF NUMBERING,

CONTAINING ALSO A GENERAL BUSINESS DIRECTORY OF THE
COUNTY OF SANTA CLARA, AND A GREAT VARIETY
OF USEFUL AND STATISTICAL INFORMATION.

COMPILED BY

W. J. COLAHAN AND JULIAN POMEROY.

First Year of Publication.

SAN FRANCISCO:

EXCELSIOR PRESS, BACON & COMPANY, PRINTERS,
No. 536 Clay Street, just below Montgomery.
1870.

CHAPTER III
The New City

Antioch had began in the late 1800's and had been fortunate that several of the founding members would live to be a part of the Twentieth Century. The City of San Jose would no longer have stables and horse and buggy would be replaced with the automobile. Another mode of transportation would be the airplane.

There would be several changes in the City of San Jose. The members of Antioch had lived through the Great Earthquake, the Chinatown fire, and they were pleased to have more African–Americans come into the City and become members of the Church.

The records indicate that Reverend Cyclades C. Laws was the first pastor of Antioch Baptist Church. He served as pastor from September, 1893 until 1895.

Reverend Thomas F. Smith would become pastor succeeding Reverend Laws in 1895. He, too, would remain for approximately two years until 1897.

According to church records, Reverend W. A. Mitchell became pastor in 1897 and he would remain as pastor into the twentieth century. His service as pastor ended in 1901.

Reverend W. Brown served as pastor of Antioch Church succeeding, Reverend W. A. Mitchell in 1901. He, too, would serve for two years until 1903.

The next pastor of Antioch was Reverend Emmett B. Reed who served three years, 1903 through 1906.

Reverend Robert A. Lewis steered the course of incorporation of the Church. His leadership was from 1906 through 1910.

In 1908, the Congregation was beginning to grow and began to think about moving in order to have a new edifice.

[1]Arbuckle

Construction of a new building on Julian Street began as the plans were approved in June of 1908. Between then and the new structure's dedication, the third Sunday in September, services were held in the hall of the Pastime Club at 315 North Tenth Street.

On the third Sunday in September, 1908, a dedication of the New Antioch was completed as planned by the congregation. Dedication day was a special day for members of the Church.

The Dedication Day began with a sunrise prayer service for the congregation and the formal dedication service took place at 3:00 p.m. in the afternoon. Reverend Robert A. Lewis remained pastor and moved to San Francisco in late 1909 or early 1910.

The new Antioch Church had a seating capacity of approximately 150 parishioners. This almost quadrupled the size of the first church.

The City of San Jose began to grow in size from 30,000 in 1890 to slightly less than 50,000 in 1910.[1]

....The Poor Saints Fund was introduced and approved.

Church Meeting Minutes
September 7, 1906

Antioch Baptist Church
Locations

First Antioch
1893 Odd Fellows Hall
1894 Sixth and Julian Streets
Second Antioch
1908 Pastime Club
1908 Sixth and Julian Streets

---

[1]San Jose Directory

The next few years there would continue to be a succession of pastors. Some had a longer tenure than others.

The first building was a city-fronted frame structure on the south side of Julian Street. The photograph of the congregation taken in 1893 has the members of the church in all of their finery of this day. The first church proved to be small and did not appear to accommodate more than forty worshippers with any degree of comfort.[1]

As the church began to grow in membership and the economic conditions improved, the members began to take steps to incorporate.

The new church had established a new pastor Reverend Doctor M. C. McIlvane in 1910. He served until 1911. Reverend J. W. Wiley then served one year from 1911 until 1912. He left Antioch and was replaced by Reverend D. L. Potts in 1912. His tenure as pastor would be three years until 1915.

Reverend J. A. Dennis would serve from 1915 until 1917 to be replaced by Reverend G. W. Hill in 1917. He would be pastor of Antioch Church until 1919.

Reverend William Allen Magette would arrive in 1920 and lead the church until 1939.

The population of San Jose in 1915, approximately 58,575, was less than 1% African–Americans.[2] The general population continued to grow, but the percentage of African–Americans remained at fewer than 1%. By 1925, there were approximately 73,167 residents of varied backgrounds and heritage.[3]

[1]Ibid
[2]San Jose Directory
[3]Ibid

....the Colored Citizens Republic Club donated $2.85 to Antioch Church. The insurance on the Church increased from $4.00 to $7.50.

Church Meeting Minutes
October 12, 1906

....Resolution of the Board of Trustees states, "$1,100 repayment of a sum secured by a mortgage."

...The Grand Rally Day will be on the third Sunday.

Church Meeting Minutes
September, 1907

Church Meeting Minutes
October 28, 1908

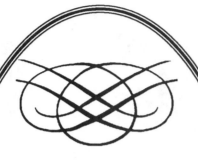

**On The Pulpit
For
Many Years**

"....Josephine Foster

married Willis Brown

December 4, 1883."

*Original Bible on the
Pulpit of Antioch Baptist Church
1894*

....the Board of Directors voted to have the Electric Bill paid for the month.

*Board of Directors Meeting
October 18, 1905*

....Reverend A. Lewis' salary was approved for $10.00.

*Church Meeting Minutes
March 9, 1906.*

✝ ✝ ✝ ✝ ✝

Reverend William Magette, Pastor, July 24, 1919, from Portland, Oregon, Mt. Olivet Baptist Church.
Age: 45
Born: January 17, 1918.

✝ ✝ ✝

*Antioch Baptist Church
Second Bible
Located on the Pulpit*

*Odd Fellows Hall
Source: Clyde
Arbuckle's San Jose*

*Below:
Hotel St. James
Source: Clyde
Arbuckle's San Jose*

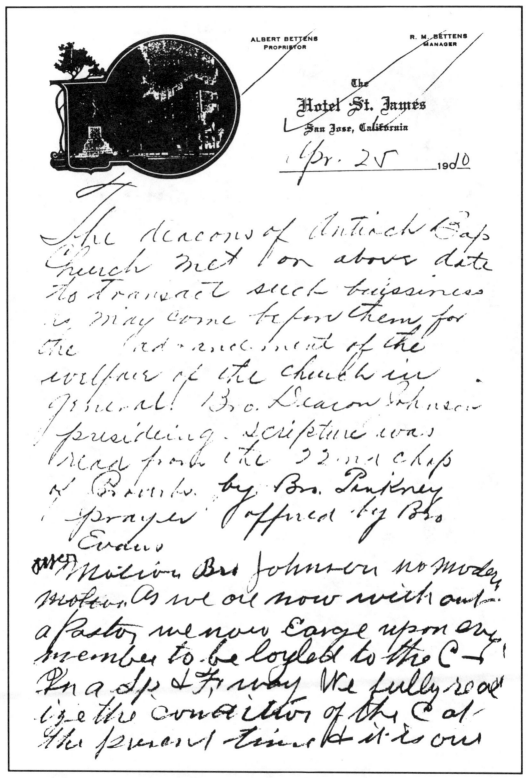

Deacon Board Meeting Minutes, April 25, 1910
Antioch Church Records

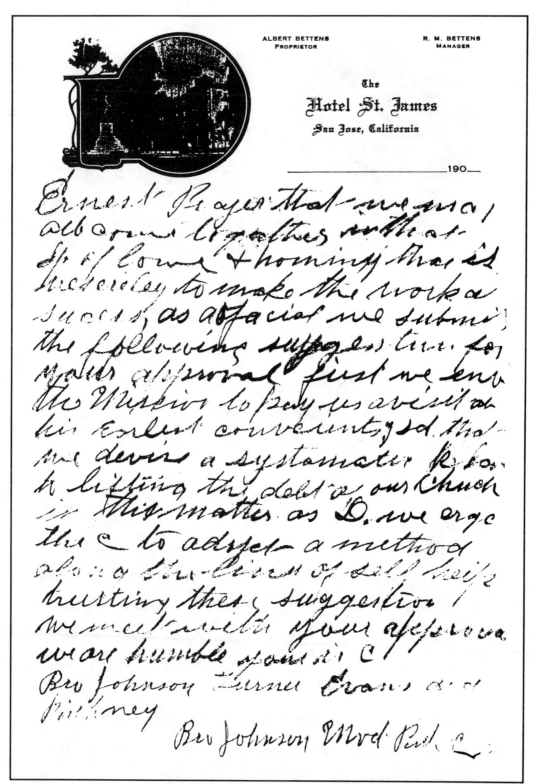

ALBERT BETTENS
PROPRIETOR

R. M. BETTENS
MANAGER

The

Hotel St. James

San Jose, California

_____ 190___

Earnest Prayer that we may all come together in the Sp of love & knowing that it behooves to make the work a success, as a [official?] we submit the following suggestions for your approval first we [urge?] the [Mission?] to pay us a visit at his earliest convenience, 2d. that we devise a systematic plan for the lifting the debt of our Church in this matter. as 3d. we urge the c to adopt a method along the lines of self help trusting these suggestions we meet with your approval we are humble yours in C

Bro Johnson Turner Evans and Pinkney

Bro Johnson Mod. Red. C.

Deacon Board Meeting Minutes, April 25, 1910
Antioch Church Records

32

Minutes of Sunday School, October 13, 1912
Antioch Church Records

The minutes of the Antioch Bapt.
S.S for Sunday October 13, 1912
School called to order by Mrs. Williams
of San Francisco at 9.50
School led in prayer by Bro. William
of Pacific Grove. A few hymns from
hymnal sung by the school.
For scripture reading First division of
Psalms was read.
Subject of lesson Clean and Unclear.
Mark. 7-1-28. Golden Text. For the
kingdom of God is not Meat and
Drink; but righteousness, and peace,
and joy in the Holy Ghost. Rom.
14. 7

Minutes of Sunday School, October 13, 1912
Antioch Church Records

City of San Jose following the 1906 Earthquake
Source: Clyde Arbuckle's San Jose

Sunday School Song Book, Circa 1915
Antioch Church Records

Reverend D. L. Potts, Pastor
Antioch Baptist Church

Reverend Williiam Allen Magette, Pastor
Antioch Baptist Church

CHAPTER IV
A Changing San Jose

Antioch Baptist Church had endured the first building 1894. This edifice had served the membership well in those early days.

On April 18, 1906, the earth shook in San Francisco with the large earthquake. The City of San Jose had its share of tremors, fires, and damage.

The Antioch Baptist Church was near the downtown area where much of the earthquake damage occurred. Much of the damage in the City was on San Fernando Street along First, Second and Third Streets.[1] There was extensive damage to the brick buildings in the area as well as fire damages. The church foundation was severely damaged resulting in a move to another building.

A special meeting of the Church membership, approved the building of another church on July 16, 1907.

A move to the Pastime Club took place. This location was located at 10th and Julian Streets.

On October 14, 1907, two contractors were interviewed to examine the foundation of the building.[2]

Photograph of
Stained Glass Window
Antioch Baptist Church

In 1908, this small band of believers would return to a new foundation with still more changes to the church.

Under the leadership of Rev. Potts, Antioch improved the front of the Church in 1914. They also began a Dollar Day Rally that would continue for many years.

---

[1]Arbuckle

[2]Antioch Church Records

Stained glass windows represented the Christian architecture of this period. The first such windows were purchased for Antioch Church by the Christian Endeavor Society.

Reverend William A. Magette served as the pastor of Antioch Baptist Church from 1920-1939. The City continued to change the congregation also began to grow.

The population of African–Americans in the City of San Jose continued to be published at less than 1%.[1]

The new church rebuilt in 1908, with a seating capacity of 150, served Antioch well for three decades. The influx of new residents during World War II soon rendered the facilities inadequate.

Reverend Magette saw the changing San Jose and served as pastor for nineteen years. The new families who came to San Jose did not see the changes as rapidly as those who had been at the Church and had watched the metamorphoses of Antioch Baptist Church.

New members, new programs, new ideas and new pastor who continued not only with the old procedures, but also planned for the future.

Photograph of
Stained Glass Windows
on the South Side of the Church

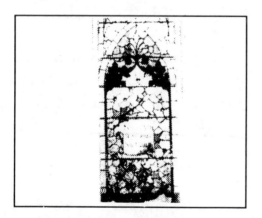

Photograph of
Stained Glass Windows
on the South Side of the Church

---

[1]San Jose City Directory, 1939

At the beginning of Reverend William Allen Magette's service as pastor of Antioch Baptist Church in 1920, it was an interesting time for African–Americans in San Jose. World War I had ended and many had left the southern states to work in the industries of the North.

Members of the Antioch Baptist Church greeted their new pastor, Reverend Magette who served them for nineteen years, longer than any of the previous pastors of Antioch Church, to date. He, too, was a part of the changes in the city and the small flock that continued to grow.

The migration of African–Americans from the south to California, and then to San Jose, had a profound effect on the Antioch Baptist Church. With this new migration came members from many cities in the south and the east.

The Garden City of San Jose, with many farms and orchards, began to see more African–Americans become permanent residents. Reverend Magette was an active pastor. Not only was the population of the church growing but church programs were changing as well.

The Antioch Church suffered during the Depression of the 1930's. There was not as much money for the church and the needs of the members and people in the community were great. Reverend Magette and his flock would continue to help the poor of the church and the City of San Jose.[1]

Even though there were hard times for the members of the Antioch Church, there were always periods of thanksgiving. One of the events that provided fellowship was the church picnic. Church records indicate that the Sunday School Picnic was an active and popular event. The picnic was often held at Congress Springs, located in Saratoga, California. This was a time for relaxation, fun and fellowship.

---

[1]Antioch Church Records

Reverend William Allen Magette passed the torch to Reverend T. M. Davis in 1940. He served as pastor of Antioch Baptist Church until 1946. He too, administered to a flock during a difficult period in the history of this country, World War II.

One year after Reverend T. M. Davis became pastor of Antioch Church, the United States became a major participant in World War II. The war began for this country with the bombing of Pearl Harbor on December 7, 1941. There was an even greater migration of African–Americans to California during and after the war. They came to work in the shipyards, government facilities, and to serve in the military.

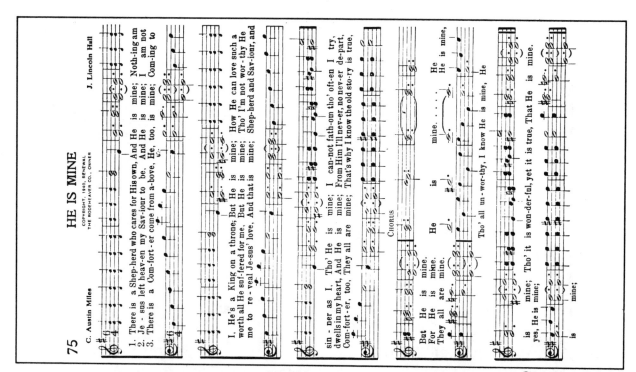

Circa: 1940
Church Hymn
Source: Antioch Church Records

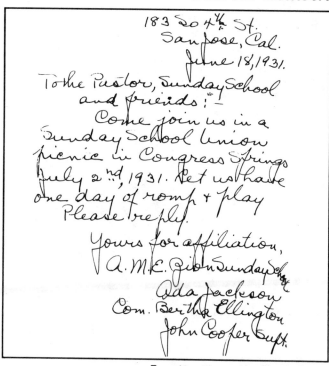

Invitation to Sunday
School Union Picnic
Source: Antioch Church Records

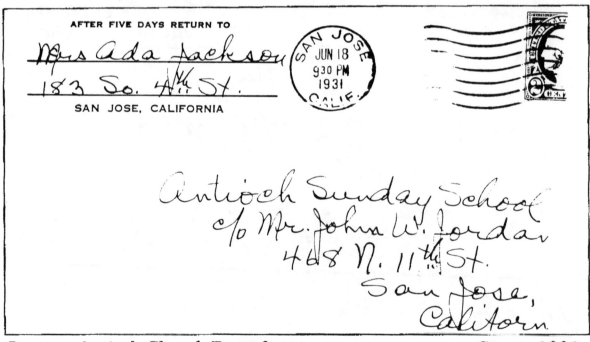

Source: Antioch Church Records   Circa: 1928

Letter from Henrietta Harris

Source: Antioch Church Records   Circa: 1931

Envelope to John Jordan
regarding Sunday School

407 Branciforte St.,
     Vallejo,Calif.

Mrs.I.Adams,
211 E.Empire St.,
San Jose,Calif.

Circa: 1938
Letter to Mrs. I. Adams
Source: Antioch Church Records

> To the Members of the Antioch
> Baptist Church. Greeting
> We the Deacons and trustees beg leave to
> make the following report.
> On Sunday April the 21st. a conference
> was held with Rev. C. W. Washington in
> regards to a call as pastor of
> the Church. after a general discussion as to
> the condition of the church and all concerned.
> Bro Washington stated he would consider the
> call. In regards to salary we agreed on
> $ per month. until something worked
> out better. Bro Washington would fill the
> pulpit from Richmond for the time being.
> We immediately notified the Missionary Bro
> Mitchell that we were going to recommend the call
> We also feel that if Bro Washington is called
> that his service began the first Sunday in
> May therefore we do recommend that
> this report is adopted.
> Respectfully Bros Chad. Davis Theo West.
> William C. Kelly.
> Rev. Moss

Circa: 1936
Call of Reverend C. W. Washington as Pastor
Source: Antioch Church Records

*Antioch Church
Picnic 1935, Congress Springs, Saratoga
Courtesy of Joyce Ellington*

*Antioch Church
Picnic 1935, Congress Springs, Saratoga
Courtesy of Joyce Ellington*

Mrs. Sargent Moss
Member of Antioch Church, 1935
Courtesy of Joyce Ellington

Rev. William A. Magette and Theodore Moss
Antioch Church Picnic, 1934
Courtesy of Joyce Ellington

45

Mrs. "Brecky" Breckenridge
Member, Antioch Church
August 18, 1931
Courtesy of Joyce Ellington

Mr. Theodore Moss and Mr. Henry Ribbs
June 29, 1935, Congress Springs, Saratoga
Courtesy of Joyce Ellington

CHAPTER V
Civil Rights Movement

In 1946, Antioch Baptist Church had a new pastor. Reverend T. M. Davis had served for several years succeeding Reverend William Allen Magette.

The entire country was soon to become involved in the Civil Rights Movement.

Antioch Baptist Church under the leadership of Reverend C. W. Washington and later the Reverend Doctor M. Samuel Pinkston would be at the forefront of many of the issues confronting African–Americans in the City of San Jose.

Antioch flourished and initial plans to create a building fund in order to purchase a larger building were completed. Reverend Magette's health went into decline and he was forced to retire.

Reverend T. M. Davis kept the dream alive by increasing the funds in the building fund. He served as pastor terminated by death after serving a brief period of time.

....200 demonstrators brave cold, rain at the Post Officio. Rev. C. W. Washington uses the Microphonic on the bed of a pick up truck to urge demonstrators to oppose the sealing of the Mississippi representatives in the U. S. Congress on Monday.

East San Jose Mercury News
Sunday, January 6, 1965

While Reverend C. W. Washington served as pastor, he was a thriving force to build another edifice of worship for the membership of the church.

On May 22, 1960, the New Church was dedicated under his leadership. The work on the church had began in August 1959, and Ella Davis the oldest member of Antioch, was present at the dedication ceremony. She had been a member of the old Antioch but had been blessed to see another Antioch built on the same site as the original church.

The New Church of stucco exterior with flagstone and redwood trim, included a Sanctuary, Chapel with a seating capacity of 625, an Educational building, Dining room, Kitchen facilities, and a Pastor's Study and office.

The dedication of Antioch Baptist Church was a project that was done through the assistance of members, family, and friends.

Rev. C. W. Washington served as a member of the Board of Directors for the Red Cross and Santa Clara County School Board. He was very active in civic and community affairs, serving as the first and only African–American member on County boards and commissions.

Statements on Dr. King:

Rev. C. W. Washington, Pastor of Antioch Baptist Church and Santa Clara County Board of Education Trustee:

The tragic killing of Dr. King in Memphis, Tennessee, is certainly a senseless act. It casts such a gloomy reflection upon a democratic society in which citizens have a right to dissent and protest

San Jose Mercury News
April 5, 1968

Antioch continued to grow and flourish and was involved in the Civil Rights Movement throughout the United States and in San Jose, California. The Sunday School and Missionary Departments had been organized in the early 1900's. This enabled the members of the church to teach the younger children and gave the missionary women the opportunity to visit and care for the sick of the church. The Poor Saints Fund continued to help the needy and the sick into the twentieth century.

The church records indicated that a Sanctuary Choir was formed under the pastorage of the Reverend T. M. Davis. He was also instrumental in organizing the church Senior Choir which changed its name to the Sanctuary Choir. This growth continued with the admission of college students from San Jose State University and parishioners new to the city.

Reverend C. W. Washington in accepting the call to Antioch came from Detroit, Michigan. He received his B.A. Degree from San Jose State University and his M.A. from Berkeley Baptist Divinity School.

He was an active pastor for the church in civic and church activities. As a member of the Santa Clara County School Board, active participant with the Red Cross, and the National Association for the Advancement of Colored People (NAACP), Antioch hosted meetings, sessions, and events.

In 1963, an All States Day was introduced to Antioch as a fund raiser for the church in order to meet the mortgage obligation. Governors for each of the United States represented in the church or a combination of states were elected and lists of members born in each state were provided for this event to the governor.

Reverend C. W. Washington contributed significantly to the success of the inception of the concept of All States Day by soliciting funds and assisting small states with their funds so that all states were representative to this project.

This concept has continued to be a major fund raiser for Antioch even today. Throughout the year, the members of each state meet independently for each of their fund raising projects and come together with their governor on All States Day. This special day continues to be held on the Sunday preceding Thanksgiving when the governors make their financial report for the year and submit names of the contributors for the church records.

Antioch continued during this period to be a staunch

advocate for civil rights with African–American organizations, Community organizations, Church groups, and Housing.

The church was an active member of the Santa Clara County Council of Churches. Records reflect monthly payment receipts in the late fifties and early sixties. A newspaper article, in which discrimination in housing was discussed, showed Antioch Baptist Church as a leader in the movement.

Antioch was the primary institution in the building and development of the San Juan Bautista Apartments located at the end of Cunningham Street in the Tropicana Village Area of San Jose. This took place through a partnership with the church and the Housing and Urban Development Department (HUD) in the late sixties. This housing development was still another demonstration that not only was the church an advocate for housing and discrimination but was willing to provide an opportunity for the low income resident in San Jose to be able to have an apartment.

An African–American church that provided spiritually to the residents of San Jose was also now providing physically in the area of housing. The church was recognized as a leader in the community and in the City of San Jose.

Antioch Sunday School Records
Circa: 1928
Source: Antioch Church Records

*Reverend T. M. Davis, Pastor
Antioch Baptist Church*

Rev. C. W. Washington, Pastor
Antioch Baptist Church

Courtesy American Baptist of the West

MAKE WAY FOR THE NEW — Final services were held last Sunday in Antioch Baptist Church ★ ★ ★ at 268 E. Julian St. and wreckers now have the building almost demolished, as shown here. In its place will rise a new sanctuary and a two-story educational building. The old church was built over 60 years ago. ★ ★ ★

Source: San Jose Mercury News
Final Services in Antioch Baptist Church

EVERYTHING G O E S — The Rev. C. W. Washington, left, pastor, takes down a banner, and Van Wilson, deacon and treasurer, prepares to remove a drinking fountain during wrecking operations at Antioch Baptist Church. Only old item so far slated for inclusion in the new building is a stained glass window. ★ ★ ★

Source: San Jose Mercury News
Reverend C. W. Washington
and Deacon Van Wilson

Civil Rights March
Source: San Jose Mercury News

Civil Rights Commemoration
Source: San Jose Mercury News

6 Wednesday, Dec. 7, 1960 San Jose Evening News

PLAN DINNER—Antioch Baptist Church's second annual fund raising dinner, expected to be attended by more than 500 community leaders, is discussed by members of the dinner committee. Seated, left to right are Wester Sweet, a San Jose attorney; the Rev. C. W. Washington, church pastor, and Supervisor Ed R. Levin. Standing is Alden B. Campen. The Rev. Mr. Washington is holding a photograph of Lt. Gov. Glenn Anderson, who will speak at the dinner.

Antioch Baptist Dinner To Be Held Saturday

Plans were being made today for Antioch Baptist Church's second annual testimonial dinner, at which the guest speaker will be Lt. Gov. Glenn Anderson.

The dinner, expected to be attended by more than 500 community leaders, will be held at 6:30 p.m. Saturday in the social hall of the Grace Baptist Church at 10th and San Fernando streets.

Purpose of the dinner is to honor the pastor of Antioch Baptist, the Rev. C. W. Washington, and to raise funds for the church's new building at 268 E. Julian St.

The new $85,000 structure was dedicated last May by Dr. Mack McCray Jr., executive secretary of the Northern California State Baptist Convention.

Reservations for the dinner may be made by calling CYpress 2-5743 or CY5-0066.

The lieutenant governor, a former assemblyman and mayor of Hawthorne, will speak on "Facing Our Responsibilities."

Source: San Jose Mercury News
Annual Antioch Baptist Church
Testimonial Dinner

The Black Church . . .
. . Agent Of Protest

Source: San Jose Mercury News
The Black Church....
Agent of Protest

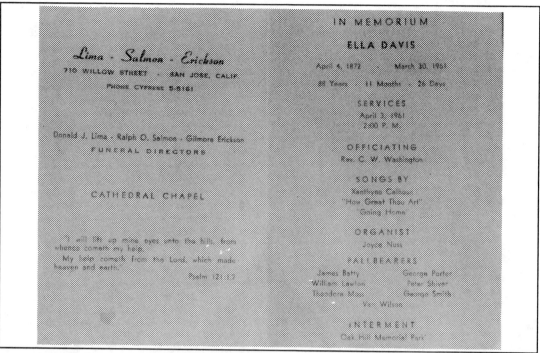

Source: Antioch Church Records

*Funeral Program
For Founder Ella Davis*

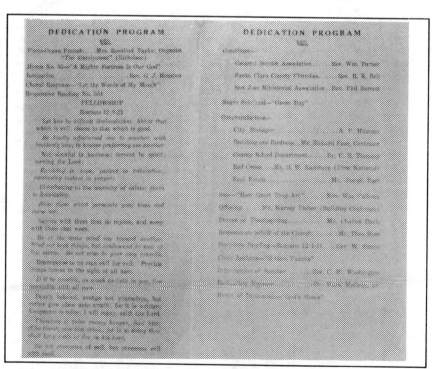

*Source: Antioch Church Records
Dedication Program*

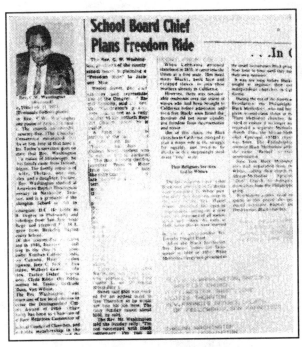

*School Board Chief Plans
Freedom Ride
Source: San Jose Mercury News*

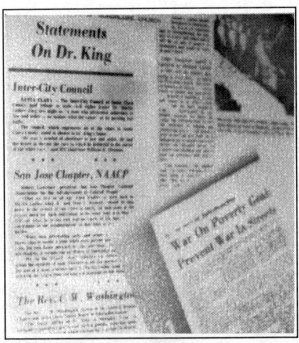

*Statements on Dr. King
Source: San Jose Mercury News*

CHAPTER VI
Urban Renaissance

In February, 1973, Rev. C. W. Washington passed the baton to the Reverend Eddie Porter. He served as the interim pastor of Antioch Baptist Church following the death of Reverend C. W. Washington.

It is interesting to note that Reverend C. W. Washington had surpassed Reverend William Allen Magette as pastor of the Antioch Baptist Church. The Church had flourished during those years.

The Antioch Church records reflect that there was an active Sunday School church treasurer, trustee board, deacon board, board of Christian education, a children's work chairperson, senior usher board, junior choir, clerk, janitor, organist, senior choir, and missionary circles. There were groups such as the Christian friendliness, spiritual life, white cross, reading and literature, sick committee, and a BYF.

In September, 1974, Antioch Baptist Church extended the call to Reverend Doctor M. Samuel Pinkston, a native of Camden, New Jersey. He was serving as Minister of Public Ministries for the American Baptist Churches of the West at its headquarters in Oakland, California.

With the assistance of several members and Reverend Pinkston, the Church Congregation was able to establish the Antioch Senior Citizens' Nutrition Program. This was a joint effort of the City of San Jose, Santa Clara County and the federal government with Antioch providing the leadership for this project. This project proved to be tremendously beneficial to seniors by providing quality fellowship enabling them to look forward to one hot nutritious meal five (5) days a week.

The seniors in the program had group outings; special trips, sewing circles, and a period during the day when they found fellowship and caring. Many were able to find spiritual solace and strength in the quietness of the sanctuary during the day. Several of the Senior Citizens' Nutrition Program participants attended the Sunday morning services of Antioch Church.

A memorable event was the employment of church secretary. Antioch continued to be an active community leader and the need to have a secretary was realized and each of the members of the church have served with honor, humility, professionalism, and distinction. There are a myriad of situations that must be completed during the day and the secretary provides the continuity for the church.

A Children's Church was organized to provide spiritual growth to the young during the morning worship service. The emphasis on young people and early childhood education was introduced enabling members and visitors to the church found a special place and service for their children.

The Mission Outreach to Haiti was inspirational for the Antioch Baptist Church. A member of the church volunteered to work on the project. With the assistance of members of Antioch Church, there was regular financial support and missionary zeal to churches in Haiti. The Mission Outreach support that Antioch Church has given has included assistance in Haitian resettlement in the community, housing, food, and clothing.

The Women's Weekend has brought interest to the women and the membership of the church. This program helped to respond to a larger view of missions, as women met in seminars and workshops with a final meeting being a worship service on Sunday.

Outreach Ministry activities included a focus on the Youth of Antioch Church. Under the direction of the leader, there were activities such as weekly Youth Bible classes, athletic events, weekend camping during the year, summer camps, ski trips, and a Youth Basketball Team. The Antioch Church Basketball Team was the Church League Championship Leaders for three (3) consecutive years. The trophies that the youth received are in the trophy case in the narthex.

Antioch Church continues to grow from the early days and the weekly program would not only give a parishioner the name and telephone number of the church but also each of the officers of the church and their home telephone numbers.

The stated meetings had grown from 1893 to include a broad list of meeting and activities for members of the church.

ANTIOCH BAPTIST CHURCH
STATED MEETINGS

Sunday Worship Services	8:00 & 10:45 a.m.	
Church School	Sundays	9:30 p.m.
Prayer Meeting/Bible Study	Wednesdays	7:30 p.m.
Church Business Meeting	Fri. after 1st Sun.	7:30 p.m
Worship Division	Sundays	Bi–Monthly
Children Church	Sundays	10:45 a.m.
Deacon Board	Mon. after 1st Sun.	7:30 p.m.
Deaconess Board	Sat. before 1st Sun.	2:00 p.m.
Senior Usher Board	1st & 3rd Tuesdays	7:30 p.m.
Youth & Jr. Ushers	2nd Saturdays	11:30 a.m.
Sanctuary Choir	Thursdays	7:30 p.m.
Inspirational Choir	Tuesdays	7:30 p.m.
Ambassadors	Wednesdays	6:00 p.m.
Crusader's Choir	Sat. before 2nd & 4th Sun.	10:00 a.m.
Helping Hands	Called	
Music Committee	Called	
Membership Development Div.	3rd Thursdays	7:30 p.m.
Church School	2nd Mondays	7:30 p.m.
Discipleship Class	Sundays	9:30 a.m.
Evangelism Committee	2nd Thursdays	7:30 p.m.
New members Committee	Called	
Nominating Committee	2nd Thursdays	6:00 p.m.
Orientation Class	Sundays	9:30 a.m.
Mission Division	2nd Tues. ea. odd Month	7:30 p.m.
Brotherhood	3rd Mondays	7:30 p.m.
American Baptist Women	3rd Mondays	7:30 p.m.
Circles: Lydia	4th Mondays	2:00 p.m.
Rosalind Jordan	2nd Mondays	2:00 p.m.
Inez Jackson	Wednesdays	9:00 p.m.
Bus. & Prof. Women	4th Sundays	4:00 p.m.
MLK–CWW Schol. Committee	Called	
Resource Division	Thursdays after 1st Sunday	7:30 p.m.
Trustee Board	4th Tuesdays	7:30 p.m.
Deacon–Trustee (joint)	3rd Tuesday (Jan., April, July & October)	
Board of Christian Education	1st Tuesdays	7:15 p.m.
Social Action Division	4th Mondays	7:00 p.m.
Youth Bible Study	1st, 3rd & 5th Sundays	5:00 p.m.

Courtesy of Antioch Baptist Church Program

One of the greatest joys of a pastor is to assist and train others for the Gospel Ministry. Reverend Pinkston found, that during his fourteen (14) years as pastor, several were licensed to preach the Gospel from Antioch and some have been fully ordained for the Gospel Ministry.

SONS AND DAUGHTERS
OF ANTIOCH CHURCH GOSPEL MINISTRY

Licensed

Nathaniel Newman
Steven Pinkston
Darius Brown
David Dill
Shirley Fisher
Ronnie Herrell

Ordained

Reverend Nathaniel Newman, presently a pastor in the area.
Reverend Shirley Fisher, presently a pastor in the area.
Reverend Steven Pinkston, presently dean of students,
     Bellarmine College Preparatory School.
Reverend Herman Kemp, former U. S. Army Chaplain,
     Captain, Active Reserves.

Reverend Doctor M. Samuel Pinkston served fourteen (14) years as pastor of Antioch Church. During the period of time that he was pastor, the ministers that have been a part of the Ministerial Team are:

Cleveland Kimble
Eddie Porter
James Batty
Willie Harris
Jean–Moise Angervil
Nathaniel Newman
Steven Pinkston
Herman Kemp
Larry Fewell
Carl Dorsey
Charles Washington
Darius Brown
David Dill
Ronald Barr
Ronald Herrell
Shirley Fisher

During his tenure as pastor, the church was completely renovated. The church debt was paid off in a short time, and a new Antioch would rise again.

Suzette Goss–Geffrard–*Zaire

A RECORD OF THE ANTIOCH BAPTIST CHURCH EDIFICE		
First Antioch	1893	Odd Fellows Hall
	1894	Sixth and Julian Streets
Second Antioch	1908	Pastime Club
		Tenth and Julian Streets
	1908	Sixth and Julian Streets
Third Antioch	1960	Dedication of New Building
		at 268 East Julian Street
Fourth Antioch	1980	Rededication of the New Building
		with remodeling of the Sanctuary
		and other areas of the Church.

*American Baptist Commissioned Missionary

Reverend Doctor Pinkston, a native of Camden, New Jersey was from a family of seven sons and one daughter. He served proudly in the United States Army as a Second Lieutenant.

Dr. Pinkston received his B.A. degree from Gordon College. His seminary work was completed at Temple University School of Theology, Philadelphia, Penn. He received a Master of Divinity degree and also a Masters of Social Work from Rutgers University, New Brunswick, New Jersey. He earned his Doctor of Philosophy degree from California Graduate School of Theology.

Reverend Doctor M. Samuel Pinkston, served as an adjunct professor at San Jose State University and San Jose Bible College for many years primarily in the areas of Afro–American Studies and Theology. He served as an assistant to the pastor, staff position with American Baptist Churches of the West, pastorates in Rhode Island, New Jersey, and Antioch Baptist Church in San Jose, California.

A member of City and County Committees, Commissioner for the County, and Dean of the Interdenominational Ministers Alliance of San Jose he remained active in the Community, County, and the City of San Jose throughout the fourteen years.

Reverend Doctor M. Samuel Pinkston retired as pastor of Antioch Baptist Church in 1988.

The church body has designated him Pastor Emeritus of Antioch. He had assisted in the remodeling of the Church as well as continuing to provide leadership to the members, the African–American Community and the City of San Jose.

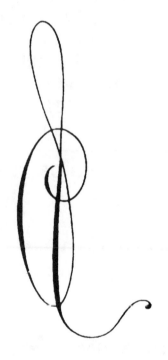

*Reverend Eddie Porter, Interim Pastor
Antioch Baptist Church*

hereas:

The Reverend Eddie Porter, our Brother in Christ, during a period of over sixteen months when the Antioch Baptist Church was without Pastoral Guidance, did answer the Challenge of maintaining our continuity of Christian Service by giving of himself freely and unselfishly, with no thought of earthly reward or to the sacrifices and personal hardships which he must have endured; and,

hereas:

Our young Associate Ministers in the persons of Reverend Gerald Johnson, Reverend Chester M. McCall, and Reverend Charles Washington Jr. III, did serve with such fervor, love and devotion that Our Savior, through them touched all our hearts, some for the first time and caused others to renew their faith and service to the Master; and,

hereas:

The Reverend James R. Davis did place himself at our disposal during this time of need, contributing greatly to this Christian effort and in so doing decided to cast his lot with us; and,

hereas:

The Board of Deacons, so ably chaired by our Brother Peter Shiver Sr., did nobly and without fear or favor so efficiently discharge the business of the Church that most members were spared the trauma of the endless, fruitless meetings and arrangements and rearrangements of programs made necessary by our bereavement; yet at the same time they did maintain the spiritual Health of the Membership, through Prayer and Devotion; and,

hereas:

The Board of Trustees, with Brother Harvey L. Fisher as Chairman did establish and maintain these priorities necessary to protect our financial status, even in the face of a dwindling budget, yet at the same time managed to successfully inspire us through prayer to even greater Christian Stewardship in our giving and sharing of time and talent.

Resolution Given To Interim Pastor Reverend Eddie Porter
Source: Antioch Church Records

Antioch Baptist Church
July 7, 1960

This Report adopted in regular business July 7, Motion by Marcell... Seconded by Dee W. Sm Carried as Presented at meeting

Rules for use of the Church Facilities;

1) We will not charge for the use of the Building, but will ask for donation, Satisfactory to the Churck.
2) Persons using the dinner room and kitchen will leave the building clean.
3) If dishes are broken by Church Auxiliaries,use them for the Church theywill be replaced by the Church, each group should report any broken
4) Cabinets are to be open for Church member and left open until the group has finisher using the Kitchen.

5) Janitor should have key for the main lock in the building.
6) A Committee of 3 women recommenened by the the womens of the Church and approved by the Church, shall be responsible for the kitchen and have keys for the cabinets.
7) When the janitor is ask to perform extra service by group using the building he should be paid by them a minimum of $5.00(for cleaning building etc.)
8) The presidents Chairmam ect. of each Auxiliaries are responsible for closing the building at the close of their meeting, see that lightsare out windows and doors are closed.
9) The Organ should be under the Direction of the Church Organist, and a key should be available for the janitor to open the Organ for visiting Churchs.

10) The date chairman should become active keep a calendar up to date, and posted where member can check for dates,

11) Telephone be change to a regular phone at $14.50 per month, put an extent phone in the hall, dropped the Minister names on the advertising.

12) Some room in the Church should be designated as a Church offic he finanice Secretary and Church clerk would have a place to store heir supplice, and used as needed for work by any member of the Church.

13) Because we now have Four class in two room and one room not ilable as a class room, the Supt. of the Sunday School would like move the class into the Sanctuary. The Men and Women's classes, so the young Adult with ok to used the Nursey if needed.

Dates for use of the Sanctuary shoul be cleared throught the tor and Deacons board, Dates for Social Hall and Kitchen should cleared through Kitchen committee and Trustee Board.

The names of the Committee that Compile the rules

Bro. G.W. Smith   Bro. Harvey Fisher
Bro. James Batty   Bro. Warren Morris
Bro. C.Davis   Bro. George Adams
Bro. T. Moss   Sis Ivez C. Jackson

The rules have ben Approved by the Deacons Board and Pastor, and we Offer these rules as an Recommendation from the Deacons Board

Charman C. Davis
Co-Ch. G.W. Smith
Pastor Rev. C.W. Washington

Rules For Use of the Church Facilities
July 7, 1960
Source: Antioch Church Records

HUNT ENGINEERING CO.
WILLIAM HUNT, MANAGER
19 NORTH SECOND STREET
SAN JOSE 18, CALIFORNIA

Mar 1 1947

Antioch Baptist Church
Julian St. bet. 6th and 7th
San Jose, Calif

Plat and Survey of Church property with
additional 17' extension in rear------------$35.00

less 50%   -17.50
Amount due $17.50

Source: Antioch Church Records
Survey Bill For Extension In The Rear Of The Church

HUNT ENGINEERING CO.
WILLIAM HUNT, MANAGER
19 NORTH SECOND STREET
SAN JOSE 18, CALIFORNIA

Property surveyed

Antioch Baptist Church
c/o Mr. Chas. Davis

San Jose, Calif

Source: Antioch Church Records
Envelope For Survey Of Church Property

268 East Julian Street
San Jose, CA
November 16, 1974

Dear Member:

We would like to take this opportunity to acquaint you with the events celebrating a new beginning of life in our church.

On Sunday, December 8, 1974, at 3:30 p.m., the installation services of Reverend M. Samuel Pinkston, as Pastor of Antioch Baptist Church, will be celebrated with Reverend Gillette O. James, Pastor of Beth Eden Baptist Church, Oakland California, bringing the installation message.

Following the services a time of fellowship will be held. Your participation in these events is imperative.

For your convenience, an envelope for your special offering for this event is enclosed.

Yours in Christ,

Pulpit Committee

William Johnson

Wm A. Johnson III (LM)
Chairman

Enclosure

WJ:lm

*Correspondence Announcing The Installation
Of Reverend Doctor Pinkston, November 16, 1974
Source: Antioch Church Records*

Reverend Doctor M. Samuel Pinkston
Pastor Emeritus
Antioch Baptist Church

Courtesy of Henry Gage
San Jose Mercury News, September 26, 1959

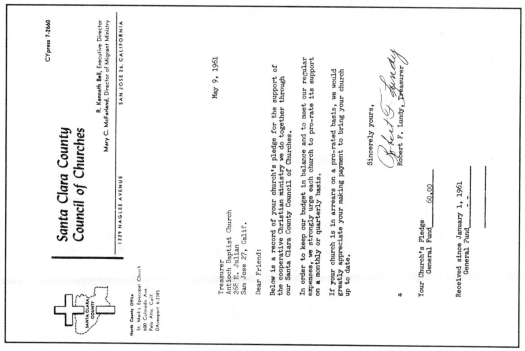

Santa Clara County Council Of
Churches Correspondence, May 9, 1961
Source: Antioch Church Records

September 28, 1961

At the last meeting of the Advisory Board held on August 21, 1961, the following recommendation was made to be submitted in the next general church meeting:

The Advisory Board of Antioch Baptist Church recommends that we accept the offer of the piano made by Brother Theodore Moss and that the money allowed in the insurance settlement for a piano, after the expense of moving, tuning & cleaning the piano, be turned over to the Trustee Board to be used toward the payment of necessary church bills at the discretion of the Board.

Warren Morris, Chairman

Submitted, Rosalind Taylor, Secretary
Advisory Board

A Gift Of A Piano To The Church
Source: Antioch Church Records

DEPARTMENT OF HOUSING AND URBAN DEVELOPMENT
FEDERAL HOUSING ADMINISTRATION
681 Market Street
San Francisco, California 94105

OFFICE OF THE DIRECTOR

IN REPLY REFER TO:

April 10, 1969

Henry C. Wong
Ass't Chief Underwriter
Multifamily
Telephone: 556-3620

Antioch Baptist Church
268 East Julian Street
San Jose, California 95112

Attention: Harvey L. Fisher, President

Re: FHA Project No. 121-35048-NP-SUP-AMP
Section 221(d)(3)
San Juan Batista Apartments
San Jose, California

Gentlemen:

Because of the depletion of rent supplement funds and the indefinite aspect of predicting the availability of such additional funds, it has become necessary for this office to discontinue the processing of your application.

You will be notified at the time funds appear to be available. If at that time you wish to proceed, this office will be pleased to accept a new application covering the proposal.

We sincerely regret the circumstances leading to this action. Should there be any questions, please call us.

All documents pertaining to the proposal will be retained by this office unless you request their return.

Sincerely yours,

Roy H. Pinkerton
Director

cc: Shanrock & Hardeman & Associates

Letter From The Department Of Housing
And Urban Development
Source: Antioch Church Records

Proposed Sanctuary: Remodeling Design
Source: Antioch Church Records

Yale University *New Haven, Connecticut 06520*

WILLIAM SLOANE COFFIN, JR., *Chaplain*

Office, 258 Durfee Hall

April 18, 1975

Antioch Baptist Church
268 E. Julian Street
San Jose, California 95112

Dear Friends,

My friends Morris Dees and Julian Bond told me you have shown your concern for Joanne Little by contributing to the Southern Poverty Law Center.

Let me congratulate you, tell you how I came to know the Center, and encourage you to continue your support of their work in the future.

In 1964 I was in Montgomery, Alabama, where city police and angry crowds had sealed me and others inside Dr. Martin Luther King's Dexter Avenue Baptist Church. A young Montgomery Police officer was stationed behind a fifty calibre machine gun atop an Alabama National Guard jeep. He kept me in his sights as I edged my way to a pay phone in front of the church to call then Assistant U.S. Attorney Nicholas Katzenbach for assistance.

Five years later, at the rural Montgomery home of one of the founders of the Poverty Law Center, this same police officer (now a city detective) stood guard outside. He was volunteering his services to protect civil rights attorney Morris Dees, his family and myself from threats f death. Morris had incurred the wrath of his neighbors by winning a court injunction preventing George Wallace from barring my delivery of an anti-war speech at Auburn University.

Both Morris and this local detective represent a changed Southern perspective, and a discussion in Morris' home that night later led to the formation of the Southern Poverty Law Center.

The detective, inside warming himself from the cold night, suggested that the real civil rights battles were yet to be fought...the battles to win equal treatment for the poor, both black and white. Morris, Julian Bond and several young Southern lawyers formed the Center a few months later. I've been astounded by what they have accomplished, not only in the South but throughout the nation.

One of their first victories integrated the all-white Montgomery YMCA, which controlled and restricted city-wide recreation to wealthy white areas. The Center obtained court-ordered paving for the streets in poor residential areas, forced George Wallace to employ black state troopers, stopped the unlawful sterilization of indigent medicaid and medicare recipients in South Carolina and Alabama, and reapportioned the 140-member Alabama legislature into novel single-member districts which resulted in the historic election of fifteen blacks plus seventy new whites from middle and low income districts.

On January 31, 1975, Center attorneys won a new trial for three young black men who had been wrongfully convicted of raping a white woman and sentenced to die in North Carolina's gas chamber.

The legal decision won by the Center in the U.S. Supreme Court have set precedents of national importance. And their work is spreading to all parts of the nation...anywhere the poor suffer injustice. In New Mexico, the Center is helping in a suit to regain treaty-granted medical care for thousands of dispossessed American Indians. A Tennessee suit funded by the Center seeks a court order requiring the state to cut the red tape that is depriving 800,000 qualified poor people of food stamps.

I think you can be proud of your support of the Center's present efforts. With the help of concerned people like you, the Center has grown and been able to bring about some very real and very important changes.

In many ways, your support came at a particularly important time because of the very thing that may have made it more difficult for you to give -- inflation. For most of us, inflation has been a serious problem, but for the poor it is a tragedy. While whatever small incomes they may have are being eaten away, the government is making drastic cutbacks in the public assistance programs which have meant at least minimal survival for so many.

Under these conditions, laws and procedures which discriminate against the poor strike with particular cruelty and harm. In Joanne Little's case, they are striking at her very life.

Joanne and many others can be grateful for your dedication. Only your concern and commitment to justice for the poor can ensure that the Center will continue to be an effective advocate of their rights.

I was there when the Center was just an idea. I've followed its progress and watched it grow. Thank you for helping to keep that idea alive. Thank you on behalf of those whose cry for help you have answered.

Sincerely,

William Sloane Coffin, Jr.

WSC:pra

Yale University Correspondence, April 18, 1975
Source: Antioch Church Records

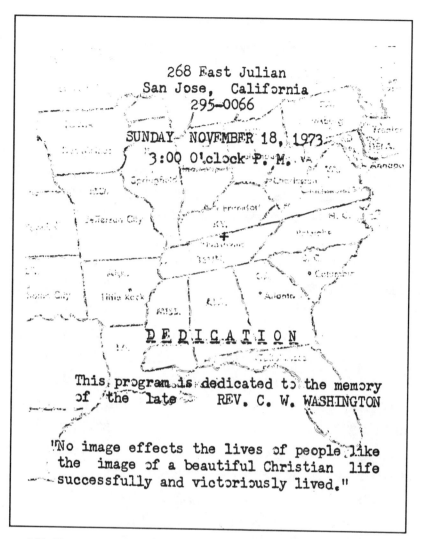

268 East Julian
San Jose, California
295-0066

SUNDAY NOVEMBER 18, 1973
3:00 O'clock P. M.

D E D I C A T I O N

This program is dedicated to the memory
of the late REV. C. W. WASHINGTON

"No image effects the lives of people like
the image of a beautiful Christian life
successfully and victoriously lived."

All States Day Program, November 18, 1973
Source: Antioch Baptist Church

CHAPTER VII
A Journey Forward

Reverend Dr. Arthur Jarrett served as the Interim Pastor of Antioch Baptist Church from 1989 until 1990. This was a journey forward for the Antioch Church.

A Pulpit Committee was formed with representatives from all segments of the Antioch Church. The purpose of the committee was to guide the selection of a new pastor for the Church.

The selection process for a pastor was a long and difficult task for the committee. They spent many long hours reviewing materials, discussing the candidates, and finalizing the search for a pastor of Antioch Church.

The process came to an end in 1990 when Reverend Frank L. Selkirk, Sr. become the final candidate and named the new Pastor.

Reverend Selkirk, a graduate of the University of Kansas with a Bachelor of General Studies, was installed as the seventeenth pastor of Antioch Baptist Church in San Jose. He had arrived in San Jose from Massachusetts with experience in the American Baptist Churches of Massachusetts. He had become one of the pastors to lead this flock which had grown since 1893. The tenure of Reverend Selkirk lasted approximately two years and ended in 1992.

The new pastor joined a group of strong leaders of Antioch Baptist Church, a legacy of proud traditions and a strong membership of African–Americans.

Antioch Baptist Church was very close to the Centennial and a period of thanksgiving, prayer, and planning was in progress in 1992.

Antioch Baptist Church has been on Julian Street between Sixth and Seventh Streets for one hundred years. The small band of Christians had grown and the children of the founders would survive earthquakes, fires, the depression, wars, racism, and many other crisis.

This recent experience was new to the members of the Antioch Baptist Church. They were faced with a situation which was painful and distressing to the membership. This was a regretable and unfortunate incident.

The departure of Reverend Selkirk was reported in the San Jose Mercury News on three Saturdays in succession. The Antioch Church endured still another crisis, the loss of a pastor. The members of the Church would cling to each other in prayer to deliberate on a replacement for Reverend Selkirk.

Reverend Richard Nance, Jr.., retired pastor of Pacific Grove, California, was selected as the eighteenth pastor of Antioch Church.

Reverend Nance had retired from his church in the fall of 1992.

He served as interim pastor until the pulpit committee completed its work in the search for another pastor.

The search for the nineteenth pastor of Antioch Baptist Church took place during the Centennial year of the Antioch Baptist Church. The journey forward continued to take place under the leadership of Reverend Nance until a replacement could be selected by the pulpit committee.

San Jose Mercury News, Saturday, February 8, 1992   Section **B**

••• c

Letters • Obituaries

Activist pastor quits after threat

By Gary Richards
Mercury News Staff Writer

It wasn't just the threatening phone call between services last Sunday or finding a dead squirrel on the porch Thursday. But those incidents, along with his inability to shake Antioch Baptist Church out of its image of a fragmented, silent and uninvolved congregation became too much for the Rev. Frank Selkirk III.

That's why the outspoken pastor of one of the largest black churches in San Jose announced his resignation as its leader at a church business meeting Friday night, ending 18 outspoken months of try-

❝I can't serve a church that doesn't want to move forward.❞
— the Rev. Frank Selkirk III

ing to forge a unity at the 98-year-old church.

"The church doesn't want to move forward, and I can't serve a church that doesn't want to move forward," Selkirk said Friday afternoon. "It's not the church I once saw having all these plans and visions."

The tro____ events of the past week also ____ a factor, said Selkirk, 39, who will stay in San Jose

and start his own church. The angry phone call came after Sunday's 8 a.m. service. The dead animal appeared on his porch four days later.

"The caller never said, 'I'm going to blow your brains out,' just that he was going to get me," Selkirk said, convinced it was a member of the congregation.

"And I suppose the squirrel could have crawled over my little 3-foot porch and died, but I don't think so."

His blood pressure shot up, worrisome for the 6-foot-5, 380-pound man who a little more than a year ago experienced scary and severe chest pains. It was not a heart

attack but his doctors warned him to take it easy.

But the hard-charging style of the self-described "amen preacher" was obvious from the first day he took the job. He blew in hard, working seven days a week and taking to the neighborhoods, knocking on doors and inviting people to Antioch. He visited prisons, and urged church members to deal with youth gangs and embrace street people with reverence.

Thursday night at a school board meeting he fought to keep black classes from being cut at Andrew Hill High School.

See SELKIRK, Page 5B

Activist Pastor Quits After Threat
Source: San Jose Mercury News

Church Sanctuary, March 1993
Source: Antioch Church Records

Reverend Doctor Arthur Jarrett, Interim Pastor
Antioch Baptist Church

Reverend Frank L. Selkirk, Pastor
Antioch Baptist Church

Reverend Richard Nance, Jr., Interim Pastor
Antioch Baptist Church

Photograph Of The Present Church
March 1993

Epilogue

Throughout this book we have looked back at our founders and the early history of African–Americans in San Jose. The view of Antioch Baptist Church in the nineteenth century was perhaps somewhat different, but also very similar.

The early founders of the church were characterized as prayerful, and Christians. They continued to look forward in their quest for a church of worship for African–Americans in the city.

The Antioch Baptist Church has not only been a place of worship, but for many, it was a place of solace, fellowship, and leadership. Each of the pastors of the church provided the growth, stability, and support in transforming the congregation. The membership of the church grew from the early founders and they left a strong Christian legacy for all of those who have followed in their footsteps.

The origins of the Antioch Baptist church were small, yet mighty. The founders were dedicated African–Americans who were successful in planting strong roots in the City of San Jose.

Antioch Church has been the recipient of gifts and visits as reflected in the church minutes. One of the many gifts during the one hundred year period was additional land. Mrs. J. R. Conner and her sister, Mrs. Helen Emmons gave, the church a gift of real estate in 1947. This was adjacent to the original site of the church.

A significant visit was when the presidential candidate Reverend Jesse Jackson came to Antioch Baptist Church. He came as part of his presidential campaign accompanied by the Secret Service and the media. This visit by Reverend Jackson was a time for rejoicing by the congregation and African–Americans in the City of San Jose.

The history of Antioch Baptist Church would not be complete without mention of Rosalind M. Taylor. She was the early author of the history of Antioch Baptist Church. She, along with Inez Jackson provided the organization of the minutes and some of the early historical documents about the church. They provided documentation and

Epilogue

order to sparse materials located in the church records. These two women have been "Keepers of the Church Records."

Antioch Baptist Church is entering the twenty-first century with a redefinition of programs. The church has been a stable force in the African–American community and the City of San Jose for one hundred years.

The church will continue to provide the influence, stability, concern, and prayer for the community. It continues to be a catalyst for the City of San Jose and African–Americans. The transformation of the building from 1893 to 1993 has been significant, but the African–Americans who make up the congregation continue to serve their God, race, and community.

Journeying Upon God's Foundations

Ephesians 2:19-22

San Jose, Calif.
Feb. 8, 1947

The Antioch Baptist Church met in a regular business meeting at 8:30 P.M. The meeting opened with devotional conducted by Pastor C.W. Washington. Scripture lesson was read from Psalms 133. Following the devotional, minutes of the last meeting were read and adopted with necessary corrections. Unfinished business was called for: Bro. Charles Davis reported that $445.00 of the Church's money had been transferred from Saving account to a Checking account. The treasure, Charles Davis and the Clerk, Inez C. Jackson's names are on the Checking account & Saving account. The names of Bro. Charles Davis, Mrs. Hazel Gordon and Mrs. Rosalind Jordon are on the Building fund. Committee Reports were called for: Mrs. Ola Ribbs, Bro. W. Lawton and Mrs. Inez Jackson, the Auditing Committee asked for an extension of time. The request was granted by the church. Mrs. Louise Lyle, one of the delegates to the Convention, made a report. Mrs. Lyle reported the Convention is asking each church to send $14.00 from the Body as a whole and not in parts from

Source: Antioch Church Records
Correspondence
February 8, 1947

Source: Author
Correspondence
November 20, 1992

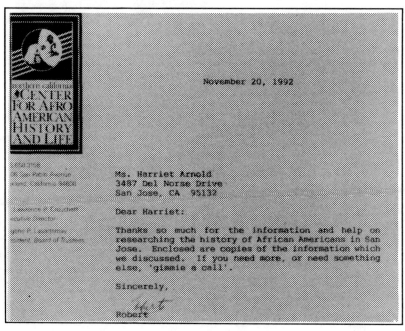

November 20, 1992

Ms. Harriet Arnold
3487 Del Norse Drive
San Jose, CA 95132

Dear Harriet:

Thanks so much for the information and help on researching the history of African Americans in San Jose. Enclosed are copies of the information which we discussed. If you need more, or need something else, 'gimmie a call'.

Sincerely,

Robert

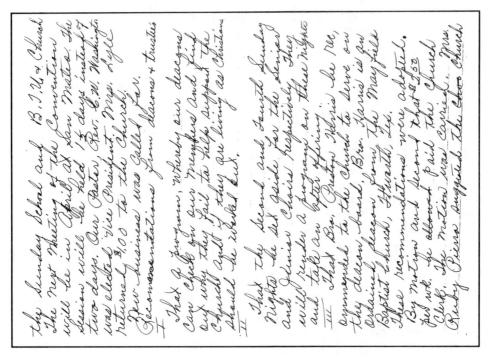

Source: *Antioch Church Records*
Correspondence
February 8, 1947

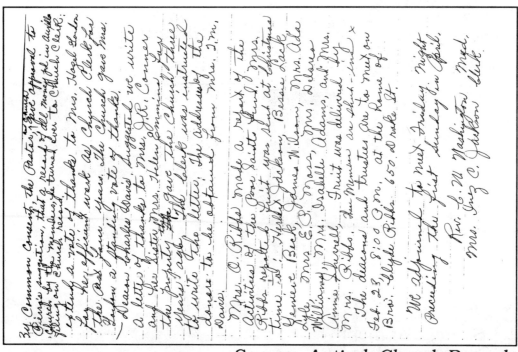

Source: *Antioch Church Records*
Correspondence
February 8, 1947

In Loving Memory Of
MRS. ROSALIND MURIEL TAYLOR

Born: January 27, 1905 Departed: February 7, 1991
California   Santa Clara, California

MEMORIAL SERVICE
Tuesday, February 12, 1991 at 7:00 p.m.

ANTIOCH BAPTIST CHURCH
268 East Julian Street
San Jose, California

OFFICIATING: Rev. Frank L. Selkirk, Pastor

Source: Antioch Church Records
Funeral Program
Rosalind Taylor

Antioch Baptist Church
268 EAST JULIAN STREET
SAN JOSE, CALIFORNIA 95112

C. W. WASHINGTON, Minister
RESIDENCE: 10560 MT. HAMILTON RD.
PHONE: 295-0066

Feb 8, 1947
Send a note to:
Mrs. J. R. Conner and her sister, (White women)
Mrs. Helen Emmons for property 17 feet
rear of the church given in memory of
Laura Jones their maid.
Laura Jones willed her property to these women

Source: Antioch Church Records
Correspondence
February 8, 1947

Source: Antioch Church Records
Reverend Jesse Jackson
with Rev. Dr. M. Samuel Pinkston and Charles Alexander

Source: Antioch Church Records
Antioch Baptist church
February, 1993 1947

Antioch Church
1893

Antioch Church
1993

Sources and Additional Notes

The primary sources used to compile the History of the Antioch Baptist Church appear in this section. There are specific areas related to this project which have primarily been church, city, interviews, memorabilia, county, and media records.

Some books were consulted for some of the chapters in this history. They include **Before the Mayflower,** by Lerone Bennett, Jr.; **Black Americans,** by Alphonso Pinkey; **A Documentary History Of The Negro People In The United States,** by Herbert Aptheker; and **Eyes On The Prize,** by Juan Williams.

Chapter One

Books:

Signposts, by Patricia Loomis; **Early Day San Jose,** by Leonard McKay; **The Negro Trail Blazers Of California,** by Delilah L. Beasley; **Ethnic Conflict In California History,** Edited by Charles Wollenberg; **Clyde Arbuckle's History Of San Jose,** by Clyde Arbuckle; **San Jose And Other Famous Places**, by Harry Farrell.

Articles:

The Rev. Peter Williams Cassey, Trinity Episcopal Church, San Jose, California; **The Antioch Journal,** Antioch Baptist Church, San Jose, California.

Newspapers and Records:

San Jose City Directory, 1893; **The Evening News,** January 6, 1893, San Jose, California; **The Evening News,** August 7, 1893; The San Jose Mercury News, January 1, 1892; **Map of the City of San Jose,** 1888, **Archives of San Jose Public Library; Antioch Church Records.**

Interviews:
Clyde Arbuckle, Historian; **Robert Hines,** Archivist.

Dissertation:

The Development And Expansion Of The Black Church In America With Special Emphasis On Northern California, by M. Samuel Pinkston.

Sources and Additional Notes

Chapter Two

San Jose City Directory, 1894; San Jose and Santa Clara County Directory, 1894; Antioch Baptist Church Records, 1893; San Jose City Directory, 1870.

Chapter Three

Newspaper and Records:

San Jose City Directories, 1890, 1910, 1915; Antioch Baptist Church Records.

Chapter Four

Newspapers and Records:

Antioch Baptist Church Records; San Jose City Directory, 1939; World Book Encyclopedia, 1985.

Interviews:

Joyce Ellington; Clyde Arbuckle.

Chapter Five

Books:

World Book Encyclopedia, 1985

Newspapers and Records:

East San Jose Mercury News, January 6, 1965; San Jose Mercury News, April 5, 1968; Antioch Journal, Antioch Baptist Church; Antioch Church Records; The American Baptist News Section of the West, September 1970; San Jose Mercury News, March 1958; San Jose Mercury News, June 11, 1967; San Jose Mercury News, December 7, 1960; Jean English Collection, San Jose Public Library, 1993; Death Record of Ella Davis, 1961.

Sources and Additional Notes

Chapter Six

Newspapers and Records:

Antioch Church Records; American Baptist Of The West Records; San Jose Evening News, September 16, 1959.

Interviews:

Clyde Arbuckle, Historian; **M. Samuel Pinkston,** Pastor Emeritus; **Eddie Porter,** Interim Pastor; **Joyce Ellington; Henry Gage,** Antioch Church Moderator.

Chapter Seven

Newspapers and Records

Antioch Church Records; San Jose Mercury News, February 8, 1992.

Sources and Additional Notes

There were several other primary sources that were used for general reference throughout this book.

Northern California Center For Afro-American History And Life, Oakland, California.
Robert Hines, Archivist, N. California Center For Afro-American History And Life
San Jose Historical Museum
San Jose Public Library, **California Room**
City of Santa Clara Main Library
African–American Community Center
Inez Jackson Library, African–American Community Center
Calvary Cemetery
Oak Hill Cemetery
Trinity Episcopal Church
American Baptist Of The West
San Francisco African–American Historical And Cultural Society
Janice Paull, Historian, Trinity Episcopal Church
Gary Banks, Mortician, San Jose, California
Joyce Ellington, Founding Family Member, Antioch Baptist Church
John Kensit, Librarian, San Jose Public Library
Rev. Eddie Porter, Interim Pastor
Joe Brown, Antioch Baptist Church
El Clausell, Antioch Baptist Church
Rev. Herman Kemp, Antioch Baptist Church
Rev. M. Samuel Pinkston, Pastor Emeritus, Antioch Baptist Church
Jean Herrell, Antioch Baptist Church
Chuck Alexander, Antioch Baptist Church
Thelma Washington, Antioch Baptist Church
Anne Stuckey, Antioch Baptist Church
Mary Fisher, Antioch Baptist Church
Mary Lou Douglass, Antioch Baptist Church
Family of George Adams, Antioch Baptist Church
Family of Inez Jackson, Antioch Baptist Church
Clyde Arbuckle, Historian, City of San Jose
Gloria Wilson, Word Processing
Nancy Balby, Assistant Archivist, San Jose Historical Museum
Leslie Masunaga, Archivist, San Jose Historical Museum
Henry Gage, Antioch Baptist Church
Family of Rosalind Taylor, Antioch Baptist Church
National Archives, Pacific Court, San Bruno, 1910, 1920
Members of the Antioch Baptist Church
Friends of the Antioch Baptist Church

Selected Bibliography

Arbuckle, Clyde and Wyatt, Roscoe D., *Historic Names, Persons and Places In Santa Clara County,* San Jose Chamber of Commerce, San Jose: 1948.

Beasley, Delilah, *Negro Trail Blazers Of California, Los Angeles, 1919,* R. And E. Research Associates, San Francisco Reprinted: 1968.

California: A Guide To The Golden State, Hansen, Harry, Editor, American Guide Series, Hasings House, Publishers, New York, Revised, 1967.

California Almanac, San Jose Mercury Newspaper, 1969.

English, Jeanne, *People and Issues, Civil Rights in San Jose, The 60's and 70's,* San Jose: 1989.

Frazier, E. Franklin, *The Negro Church in America,* Schocken Press, New York: 1964.

Goode, Kenneth G., *California's Black Pioneers, A Brief Historical Survey,* McNally and Loftin, Publishers, Santa Barbara, California: 1974.

Hall, Frederic, *History of San Jose,* A. L. Bancroft and Company, San Francisco: 1871.

Handbook Of Political Statistics of Santa Clara County Compiled for the Public Records and Newspaper Files from the Organization of the County, Pioneer Book and Job Printing, San Jose, 1878.

History of Black Americans In The West, *The Black Frontier, New Americans,* Channel 32, February 6, 1993.

Selected Bibliography

History Of Santa Clara County, California, With Biographical Sketches, Historic Record Company, Los Angeles: 1922.

Holy Bible, *Authorized King James Version, Heritage Edition,* International Bible Inc.,: 1977.

James, W. F., and McMurry G., *History Of San Jose,* Smith Publishing, San Jose: 1933.

Jenkins, Velesta, *White Racism And Black Response In California History, Ethnic Conflict In California History,* Charles Wallenberg, Editor, Tinnon–Brown, Inc., Los Angeles: 1970.

McKay, Leonard, *Postcard Memorabilia,* San Jose: 1993.

Miller–Rocq, Margaret, *California Local History,* Second Edition, Stanford University Press, Stanford: 1970.

Minutes of Church Meetings and Proceedings of the Antioch Baptist Church.

Minutes of the Sunday School of the Antioch Baptist Church.

Minutes of the Missionary Society of the Antioch Baptist Church.

Monroe, J. P., *History Of Santa Clara County, California.*

Muller, Kathleen, San Jose, *City With A Past,* The Rosicrucian Press, San Jose: 1988.

Myers, Joan de Lisle, Trinity Historian May 1974, *A Preliminary Report On St. Phillip's Mission School And The Reverend Peter Williams Cassey.*

Oak Hill Memorial Park Records (Formerly San Jose Cemetery).

Selected Bibliography

Ridout, Lionel V., *The Church, The Chinese and the Negroes in California, 1849–1893*, June 1959, Historical Magazine of the Protestant Episcopalian Church, pp. 115-138.

San Jose Bicentennial Commission, *A Century Of Service*, Smith–McKay Printing, San Jose: 1977.

San Jose Blue Book, 1903-04, *San Jose: 1904*.

San Jose Mercury News, *Centennial Edition*, June 15, 1951.

Selected San Jose City Directories 1892 through 1970, Polk–Husted Directory Company, San Jose.

Selected editions of the San Jose Mercury News; San Jose Evening News; San Jose Daily Hearld, and the San Jose Pioneer.

Snyder, David L., *Negro Civil Rights In California: 1850*, California State Archives, Sacramento Book Collectors Club, 1969.

Statements, letters and documents of events which directly and indirectly affected the Antioch Baptist Church.

Thompson, Warren, *Growth And Changes In California's Population*, The Haynes Foundation Publishers, Los Angeles: 1955.

Thurman, Odell A., *The Negro In California Before 1890*, A Thesis, College Of The Pacific, 1945, A. And E. Research Associates Reprint, Saratoga: 1973.

Thurman, Sue Bailey, *Pioneers Of Negro Origin In California: San Francisco*, Acme Publishing Company, 1949.

Wahlberg, Nestor and McKay, Leonard, *A Postcard History Of San Jose*, Memorabilia of San Jose, San Jose: 1992.

Editorial Credits

The publication of this history of Antioch Baptist Church was a long and arduous task. In order to prepare the manuscript for publication, I was reminded that the use of non–specialized jargon would not be appropriate for this book. I took the advice and the preparation was much easier to write and to collect the materials necessary for the book.

The lack of research assistants on the project required that I read and study the history of San Jose and all of the materials of the Antioch Baptist Church. In preparing the manuscript, I found that I often would retrace my steps and call on the many members of the church, friends of the church, and those who were profoundly interested in a book on early African–American Christians in San Jose.

There was an abundance of material and I received assistance from several sources. It was very difficult not to be "side–tracked" and take a different path. There was so much support that was offered freely as I researched the manuscript.

The dedication of my husband, John, my son, Jason, my spiritual family, Gloria Wilson, Gloria Weddington, Rev. Dr. Pinkston, Charles Alexander, and the members of the Antioch Baptist Church was exceptional. The patience of the publisher when things seemed to fall behind schedule was short of amazing. I thank each of you because you deserve the credit for this publication.

A special thank you to the Antioch Baptist Church for the funding of this book.

If there are faults with this book, let them lie with the author. I am indebted to everyone who made this dream a reality.

Harriett Arnold
San Jose, California

Index

A

B

C

D

Index

E

Ellington, Joyce, 44; 45; 46.
Emmons, Helen, 83.
Ephesians, 84.
Estevancio, 1.
Evans, R. J., 22.
Evans, Robert, 16.

F

Fallie, Annie, 17.
Farrell, Harry, 8.
Foster, Josephine, 29.
Fox, Frances, 12; 24.
Funeral Program, 87.

G

Gage, Henry. 71.
Gold Rush, 3.
Grand Rally Day, 28.

H

Harris, Hennrieta, 42.
Hawkins, Ella, 4; 5; 16; 20.
Hawkins, Henry, 5; 16; 22.
Hotel St. James, 30; 31; 32.

J

Jackson, Inez, 83.
Jackson, Jesse, 83.
Jarrett, Arthur, 76; 79.
Johnson, George, 17.
Johnson, Hattie, 17.
Johnson, W., 16.
Jordan, John W., 16; 42.

Index

L

Mc

M

N

O

P

Index

R

Reed, Emmett B., 25.
Reno, Willie, 17.
Resolution, 23; 28; 66.
Ribbs, Henry, 46.

S

San Jose City Directory, 5; 7; 14; 18; 24; 38.
San Jose Evening News, 5.
San Jose Mercury News, 6; 47; 71; 77; 78.
San Jose Patriot, 3.
San Juan Bautista Apartments, 50.
Selkirk, Fank L. Sr., 76; 77; 80.
Simms, Josephine, 17.
Smith, Harriett, 3; 20.
Smith, Thomas F., 25.
Sons and Daughters, 62.
Spain, 1.
Speight, H. E., 4; 20.
Sunday School, 41; 50.

T

Taylor, Rosalind M., 83.
Trinity Episcopal Church, 4.
Turner, Simon, 16.

W

Waelker, L., 16.
Washington, C. W., 43; 47; 48; 49; 52; 54; 59.
White, Alfred, 4; 20.
Whiting, William, 4; 20.
Wiley, J. W., 27.
Williams, James, 4; 20.
Wilson, Van, 54.

Y

Yale University, 74.

Z

Zion African Methodist Episcopal Church, 4; 6.

My Historical Moments
At Antioch Baptist Church

My Historical Moments
At Antioch Baptist Church

My Historical Moments
At Antioch Baptist Church

My Historical Moments
At Antioch Baptist Church

My Historical Moments
At Antioch Baptist Church

My Historical Moments
At Antioch Baptist Church

Platinum Page

Ruth R. Aladen

Charlene Alexander

Charles and Saphrona Alexander and Family

Maude A. Avery

Floyd, Jacquelyn and Shawneequa Badger

Ron & Bonnie Bane

Mrs. Daisy Boyd

Vannette, Rodney, Erica and Reginald Braddock

Robert L. & Hattie B. Bronson and Family

Joe H. & Essie P. Brown

Leola Brown

Mickelin Burnes—Browne; Awnica and April Browne

Otis & Pernina Burke

Norris & Dorothy Choice

Edward, Valia, Kenny and Sharra Clausell

Voncyle Copeland

Gladys W. Daniels

Ronald Lee and Fannie Marie Davis

Mary Lou Douglass

Grace Sypert Echols

Platinum Page

Leon E. & Wygenia Evans and Family

Harvey L. & Mary I. Fisher

Cowander V., Sabrina V. and Jennifer C. Gage

Henry Sr. & Gennie Vee Gage

Lloyd E. & Caroline J. Harris–Chambers

Arthur B. Crumpler

John & Marthelia Hargrove

Maud Henderson

Jean, Belinda, Ronnie and Gina Herrell

Donald & Audrey Holbrook

Eddie, Shirley, E. Lamont and Sharlene Jones Family

Luarthur & Patricia A. Spann Jones

Christine, Brett C., Stuart C. and Ingrid C. Johnson Family

Ms. R. Jacqueline Johnson and Family

Deacon John and Deaconess Josephine Johnson

Nellie W. Johnson and Brian Alan Johnson

The Jacksons: Arthur, Bettye, Jane, Robyn, Monte, Brittany, Evan and Nathan

The Kelly Family: Rose, Marie, Patience and Trecia

Platinum Page

Mrs. Frances Alexander King

Rev. Herman & May Kemp and Family

Oscar, Yvonne, Wesley and Erica Kyles

Lueberdia Lee and son, Lawrence W. Lee

Bobby & Petrina Lister and Family

Master Sgt. Paul K. Little

Juanita, Gregory and Terry Luster, Stephanie and Myron Naylor

Joseph & Senobia, Reginald, Cynthia, Antonie and Corky Martin

Paul and Threatta Matthews

Deaconess Nettie Earl McCalebb

The Verges, Grady and McElroy Families

Junius & Melba Shriver–McKelvey and Family

John H. & Jesie M. Mosier

Rev. Richard Nance Jr. and Family

Helen M. Norman

Roosevelt, Faye, Shanna and Terrence Norman

Harold, Sarah, Tiffani, H. Joseph III and Natalye Pearson

Frank, Johnnie, Michel and Chauvin Presbury

Isaac L. & Mary A. Ragsdale

JoVon Ragsdale

Barney & Joyce Randolph

Platinum Page

Lee Thompson & Rose Ross

Werner, Carolyn and Andrea Schultz

Ms. Debra Sharp, Jeoffrey Varner and Maurice Sharp

Ethlin Silas

Mrs. Lucille Smith

Robert, Catherine, Robert A. and T. D'Arcy Sweat and Family

Roger & Carolyn Stewart

William & Millie Stewart

Peter Sr. & Louise G. Shriver

Lester & Anne Stuckey

Richard, Carol, Miya and Zakiya Sullivan

Jessie M. Stokes

Claude, Elaine, Toniesha, Nikkema and Claude IV Taylor Family

Richard, Phyllis, Wesley and Rodney Terrell

Mildred Crumpler Thompson

Luther & Alberta Washington and Family